Public Relations Management

in

Colleges, Polytechnics and Universities

Clive Keen and John Greenall

HEIST Publications

13 West Bar Banbury OX16 9SD
☎ Banbury (0295) 68158

Acknowledgements
Thanks are due to the following for giving permission to reproduce their logos: The Automobile Association, Birmingham Polytechnic, Bishop Grosseteste College, Bovis Homes Limited, British Railways Board, Buckinghamshire College of Higher Education, The College of St Paul and St Mary, Cranfield School of Management, Coventry Polytechnic, Derbyshire College of Higher Education, Durham University, Exeter University, Hatfield Polytechnic, Keele University, Kentucky Fried Chicken (Great Britain) Ltd, King Alfred's College, Leicester Polytechnic, Mount Saint Vincent University, North Staffordshire Polytechnic, The Open University, Oxford Polytechnic, Oxford University, Prudential Corporation, Sunderland Polytechnic, Thames Polytechnic, The University of East Anglia, and The University of Wales Institute of Science and Technology.

Acknowledgement is also given to the Royal Oak, Tingewick, where the authors refreshed their ideas on many occasions.

Cover design by Richard Hoyle
Main text set in Times Roman 10 pt on 11
Composed (including typesetting codes) on an Amstrad PCW8512 and PC1512, photoset by Wordstream, and printed by McLays, Cardiff

ISBN 0 9512803 0 9

Cartoons by *Larry*

Foreword by Christopher Ball

About 14% of those aged 18 are currently admitted to higher education. The number of 18-year-olds will have dropped by some 30 percent between 1984 and 1996. These two facts, in combination, mean that

either there will be substantial reductions in higher education between now and 1996 (including widespread closure of courses, together with the merging or closing of a number of institutions), *or* the "deficit of traditional students" must be, partly or wholly, made up for by increased recruitment of mature students, the development of continuing education, and the provision of wider access for "non-traditional" 18 year-olds — such as women,[†] the ethnic minorities and the lower socio - economic groups. For persuasive social and economic reasons, but perhaps above all because of the growing need for skilled brainpower in the world of work, the Government has revised its policy on access to higher education from the first, towards the second, alternative set out above. I believe that it was right to do so.

In the future, therefore, UK higher education — or, at least, large parts of it — will experience a shift from a seller's to a buyer's market. Universities, polytechnics and colleges will increasingly be in competition with each other for students, with a corresponding reduction in student competition for access to higher education. Marketing of courses will become a key activity.

According to a recent report,[‡] "attitudes to marketing vary widely . . . partly because it means different things to different people. There is a widespread distaste for the 'hard sell' that aims to persuade people to use a service they neither need nor want. But construed more broadly marketing means the ability to view institutional activities from the standpoint of the student and employer . . . . We believe that institutions — managers and staff alike — should be more confident in promoting their achievements and their educational, academic, cultural, economic and social contributions to society. There is therefore particular scope

4

for managers to improve their skills in, and awareness of, public relations."

As a signatory of the report, I am fully persuaded of the importance of good public relations in higher education. The support it can give to marketing cannot be overestimated. But public relations is more than simply a handmaiden of marketing. Just as management is not a wholly separate activity within education — good educational management is one aspect of good education — so public relations is not separable from management. It is one aspect of good management. I have no doubt that in the changing world of higher education, effective public relations, as an integral part of an enlightened management lifestyle, will be essential to the success of individual universities, polytechnics and colleges, as well as to higher education as a whole. I am therefore particularly pleased to introduce and commend this book.

Christopher Ball

†Women "now account for about 44% of full-time students in higher education compared with less than 40% seven years ago." *Higher Education: Meeting the Challenge*. Cm 114, April 1987, page 5.

‡*Management for a Purpose*, the report of the Good Management Practice Group, NAB, March 1987, page 20.

Contents

Some definitions. Potential discord between PR and the college ideal. The nature of PR and its role in HE. The value of sound PR practice. The function of the PRP. Demystifying the role of the PR office.

Basing the programme on sound research. The need to clarify purposes. Aims, goals, and objectives.

Main targets of most college PR programmes: increasing application levels; helping the college become better known; gaining an enhanced reputation; influencing decision-makers; improving internal communications; being seen to be a good neighbour; developing beneficial alumni relations. Measuring success.

A list of audiences. How important is each? How easily are they reached? What is the impact of a college message on them? A formula for measuring overall audience ratings. The goals/audience matrix.

An overview of some of the main tools of the college public relations practitioner: media liaison, publications, exhibitions, visits, speakers' panels, audio-visual material, and advertising. The PRP as general adviser.

The PR audit: analysing the current PR strengths and weaknesses, identifying needs, and making recommendations. Optimising the goal/activity match.

The evolution of the programme over time. The PR hierarchy of needs. Planning the annual flow of work. A sample PR calendar and activity chart.

General reflections on budgeting. Four methods of allocating funds: the PR/advertising mix; matching the competition; deciding what the college can afford; management by objectives. Potential ethical problems. Establishing PR codes. General guidance on cost levels.

Preface

In the six years before this book was written a strange thing happened in the higher educational institutions of Britain. As a result of government financial policy, severe economies had to be practised by all. This was not simply a case of saving on the paper clips or turning down the heating controls. Departments were closed, student services were reduced, courses were axed, colleges merged with each other and staff were encouraged to retire early. Yet throughout all this misery the breed of public relations officers multiplied. Existing PR departments expanded and new appointments were made where there had previously been none. Public relations, however ill-defined or misunderstood, was openly acknowledged as important for the survival and progress of higher education.

In a few cases the broad corporate affairs role was envisaged for the appointees; in most, college commitment to do something was satisfied by making a fairly low-level appointment and restricting the incumbent to a limited range of duties. These duties were not expected to include advice on corporate policy matters.

The practice of public relations generally has come a long way since the early days of forty or fifty years ago when it was simply a fancy name for achieving favourable press publicity. Yet its modern meaning – and the benefits it can bring to an organisation and to society – are still not fully appreciated, even by those who are paying for the services of its trained practitioners. Indeed many practitioners themselves have been content to soldier along well-worn trenches rather than to go over the top and capture new territory for their paymasters.

It is primarily for people in higher educational institutions, whether they are employers of public relations professionals or whether they are PR practitioners themselves, that this book is written. We, the authors, believe that much of the present PR resource in these organisations is being underused because there is an imperfect understanding of the true potential of professional public relations.

Our intended audience, therefore, is as much the vice-chancellor, principal or director as it is the public relations manager, information officer or communications director. The book should also be of value to those working in cognate areas such as planning, marketing, admissions or personnel.

The examples that we use are drawn from British higher education but the principles of public relations are universal. It will be relatively easy for non-educationalists in Britain and in other countries to understand the principles being discussed and to apply them to their own circumstances. We believe that while education can learn much from the practice of public relations in commerce and industry, the book contains some original analysis which should not be confined to the world of higher education.

Throughout this text we emphasise the importance of two-way communications. Accordingly we warmly welcome any comments or suggestions that you, the reader, may have about what we have written. Letters may be addressed to us at HEIST, 13 West Bar, Banbury, Oxfordshire.

31 October 1987

9

A Note on Terminology

Titles used in British higher education tend to vary widely, and thus the authors have made use of certain terms which are intended to be read as generic:

College, for instance, is used to cover universities, polytechnics, and institutes of higher education, as well as organisations with the term "college" in their title.

Directorate is the term used to describe the college's most senior management team. In the polytechnic and college sector, it would cover the director, chief administrative officer, and deputy and assistant directors. In a university it would embrace the vice-chancellor, pro-vice chancellors, deans, and secretary or registrar.

Principal is the generic term for heads of colleges, though they may individually be entitled *vice-chancellor, director, rector, president*, or whatever.

Public Relations Practitioner (PRP) is the term used for the individual in charge of the college's day-to-day public relations activities. Such individuals currently practise under a plethora of banners, such as "head of external affairs", "information officer", "public relations officer", "director of communications", or even "deputy academic secretary". The variety does not simply reflect the usual inability to agree on titles: the work performed, and level of responsibility exercised, varies greatly between colleges, and sometimes different aspects of the job are performed by different individuals, often with no central co-ordination. The public relations practitioner as described in this book, though, does not deal just with publications, or with the media, or with exhibitions, ceremonials and hospitality, or with some other specific aspect of PR work. Rather, he or she will deal with public relations in the round. It requires the rest of this book, however, to explain precisely what is meant by "public relations in the round".

Chapter 1. Public Relations: Its Place in Higher Education

Some initial definitions

A hallowed tradition of books on PR is to start with definitions of the subject. Being great respecters of traditions, we shall do likewise:

1. Public relations is the process of persuading journalists and a hostile public that something rotten-smelling is really quite sweet.

2. Public relations is the procedure whereby half-truths are purveyed to the half-asleep to prevent their awakening.

3. Public relations is an activity involving the consumption of alcohol with the aim of persuading people to support dubious causes.

Such definitions, of course, are nonsense, and yet the nonsense remains instructive. Though few would articulate the view, a high proportion of the educated public takes it for granted that such definitions get to the essence of PR. The term *public relations* has slipped into common parlance at many points, and yet tends to be used, more often than not, in derogatory expressions such as "that's only a public relations exercise."

Starting off with definitions is usually important to authors of PR texts mainly because "public relations" can have many meanings to many people. If authors do not, therefore, state at the outset what particular meaning they attach to the expression, their subsequent arguments run the risk of being interpreted according to a conflicting view of the subject. A book on public relations within higher education, though, has an even more compelling need to be clear on this point. Higher education is concerned with tracking down, and disseminating, truth: the pursuit of truth, indeed, is almost the only ideal on which those in higher education agree. If public relations is hostile to this goal − and if the three definitions given above really do get to the heart of public relations − then professional PR practice can have no lasting place within the college.

The Institute of Public Relations nevertheless has, as one item of its code of conduct: "A member shall have a positive duty at all times to respect the truth and in this regard not to disseminate false or misleading information knowingly or recklessly and to use proper care to avoid doing so inadvertently." Honesty, in other words, is seen by the Institute as essential for the practice of public relations in any sphere; this must cause us to think twice about assuming that colleges are alone in being squeamish about small points like truth.

One definition which, though imperfect, will help to explain why public relations work is not out of place within higher education, runs as follows:

> Public relations practice is the process of organised two-way communication between an institution and its audiences; its objective is to build a level of mutual understanding and respect which allows the institution's goals to be more readily met.

An analysis of the key terms of this definition will go a long way towards providing an understanding of the subject, showing meanwhile why the usual distrust of PR is misplaced.

Communication. This is an essential part (though only a part) of public relations. But successful communication is concerned with the removal of ignorance, not its imposition. To that extent, public relations practice is wholly concordant with the college ideal rather than its enemy.

Organised. When communication involves a large institution and a number of interested audiences, it is unwise to leave it to chance and the grapevine. Just as it makes sense for functions such as personnel to be guided by specialists when an organisation reaches a certain size, so does the need for effective communication call for the specialisms of the public relations office.

Two-way. Successful public relations practice is not simply a matter of conveying information; as with all effective communication, it involves listening. And if an organisation is to deserve a sound reputation, then the response to unpleasant, but just, criticisms must be to scrutinise the behaviour of that organisation. Sound public relations practice, in other words, does not drown criticisms in complimentary gin and tonic, but seeks them out with a view to recommending corrective internal action.

To build a level of mutual understanding and respect which allows the institution's goals to be more readily met. Herein lies the crunch for the sceptics. What if the institution does not deserve to achieve its goals, because the goals are themselves dubious? What if the public relations practitioner (PRP) works for the National Front, or the government of South Africa, or a tobacco corporation? Does this not indicate that public relations is a profession of which we must remain profoundly suspicious, since part of its role might be to convince us that night is day?

This issue is tackled at several points in this book. Later in this chapter, for instance, where the nature of the PRP's tasks is discussed, it will be shown that there are no arcane means by which the public relations profession secretly manipulates opinions. Good public relations are dependent on the organisation *deserving* to be treated with respect; PRPs who work for organisations not deserving respect, and unwilling to change their ways, have an ultimately hopeless task. It will also be shown, particularly in Appendix 2, that enlightened self-interest pushes the effective public relations practitioner firmly towards sound ethical behaviour rather than away from it. In practice, college PRPs can feel confident that their work is socially beneficial rather than damaging; critics who look upon the appointment of PR personnel as lowering the tone of the college are sadly misinformed about the nature of the work and its role in higher education.

More on definitions

The definition given on the previous page has a number of merits, not least that it allows several central points to be made about public relations activity. The definition does, however, heavily emphasise the communications aspect of public relations practice. The underlying postulate is that misunderstandings, prejudice and opposition frequently stem from a lack of knowledge: if we improve the knowledge through better communications, then the misunderstandings, prejudice and opposition will evaporate. This doesn't always happen in practice, of course, but the authors have seen sufficient evidence of it in their own experience to know that the postulate has a high degree of validity. The greatest obstacle to effective public relations where higher education is concerned, certainly, is ignorance, which can be reduced through effective communication.

Nevertheless, public relations practice is not *just* about communications. As Jon White, senior tutor in public relations at the Cranfield School of Management, says, "the practitioner has a role beyond that of the communicator, a role which includes tasks of social analysis and knowledge of effective intervention and negotiation techniques".[1]

Communication is not an end in itself, but a tool. The PRP deploys communications to achieve specific purposes, and it is essential to be clear about those purposes. A skilled analysis of attitudes, and careful formulation of goals, needs to underlie any communications programme. Only a thorough understanding of what one wants to achieve through communications at any one time will allow an efficient determination of *what* is to be said, *who* should say it, *when* it should be said, *how* it should be said, *where* it should be said, and to *whom* it should be said.

A public relations programme which is internally consistent and makes maximum use of resources *must* be perfectly clear about its objectives, and thus public relations practice must be closely connected with various elements of the organisation's strategic thinking. For this reason, any definition which focuses just on communication must be too narrow, and a more general formula has to be adopted. The following definition, which was first formulated by the Institute of Public Relations in 1948, and has since withstood many attempts at improvement, serves adequately:

> Public relations practice is defined ... as the deliberate, planned and sustained effort to establish and maintain mutual understanding between an organisation and its public.

This formula cannot, nevertheless, conclude the discussion of definitions. The term "public relations" might continue to cause confusions because it has two quite distinct senses, both of which are legitimate, and both of which will be used in this book. (It is the difference between the various senses that necessitates awkward switching between "public relations *is*" and "public relations *are*".) Confusion can be reduced, though, through a distinction between *public relations practical* and *public relations absolute*. "Public relations practical" is the sense of "public relations" understood whenever we talk about public relations activities. "Public relations absolute" concerns how at any one time an organisation stands in relation to other organisations or individuals. How is it regarded by them? How does it regard them? How well or badly are the organisation and its publics disposed towards each other? Do they respect and understand each other? Do they listen or do they

14

face each other with open mouths and closed ears? Do they make allowances when something goes wrong or do they capitalise on each other's mistakes? Do they assist or obstruct each other? This sense of public relations has led the Institute of Public Relations to a second definition:

> Public relations is the state of mutual understanding between an organisation or individual and any groups of persons or organisations, and the extent and quality of the reputation that exists.

In the absolute sense it is true to say that every organisation has public relations. No organisation works in isolation. It operates in a business and social environment. Its public relations (absolute) are the sum total of its relationships with the various parts of the environment. For a college, the environment is made up of many parts: for example other colleges, local authorities, central and local government, teachers' unions, students, the local community, and suppliers of equipment. These other bodies and groups are referred to as the college's "publics", and are examined in some detail in Chapter 4.

The importance of identifying the publics and considering relations with them is twofold. If there are good public relations then the college is more likely to have the help and support of other groups in carrying out its normal functions of teaching, research, and administration. If public relations are bad then obstruction, interference and interruptions will mar the college's progress. For the college itself, good public relations will mean that it will only make and carry out policies that are in the public interest. It will be a responsible element of society and be *recognised* as such.

Public relations are affected in at least some way by everything the college does. Every letter that goes out (or remains unanswered), each public speech, the appearance of buildings, the attitudes of porters, drivers and receptionists, the actions of principals, academics and administrators: they all add to or detract from the goodwill that exists between a college and one or more of its audiences. Most of these actions, of course, happen without a consciousness of their public relations effects. But a college that understands the benefit of having good public relations and wants to do something about it can certainly do so.

The value of sound PR practice in higher education
The above, it is hoped, has begun to clear the air a bit, but there may still be some doubts about the relevance of the public relations practitioner to higher education. Isn't paid PR only really necessary in

business, where one must go to considerable lengths to acquire a favourable reputation for one's company and products?

Before 1981 lots of people in higher education used to believe that. It was, they thought, patently obvious to everyone why higher education mattered. Universities, polytechnics and colleges had a divine right to a couple of billion pounds a year of taxpayers' money. The events of the eighties have swept away this sort of complacency. Higher education had been quite well funded by the government during the sixties and seventies but that came to an end when, in the early eighties, universities, polytechnics and colleges became a target of the Government's attempt to reduce public expenditure. The institutions were dismayed and turned to society for support in a fight against the cuts. But with few exceptions the support, which was thought to be widely available, proved to be a figment of the colleges' collective imagination. The cuts took place. Colleges were closed or merged, departments disappeared, staff were shed. The goodwill that should have been built up in previous years was seen not to be there in sufficient quantity. This crisis, whatever its costs in other respects, altered colleges' own views about the importance of public relations. It is now realised that higher education is almost wholly dependent upon the goodwill of voters and their representatives. If colleges are not perceived as "good things worth supporting", then the money just will not be forthcoming. Ironically, commercial organisations are in fact far less, not more, dependent upon the goodwill of the general public, because their income is rarely derived so exclusively from the public's elected representatives.

Society as a whole finances the higher education system, but in the UK, so far, only a relatively small proportion of the population has benefited directly from it. The colleges have a positive duty to be accountable to the public; the public has a positive right to know how its money is being spent. Colleges that think of themselves as remote from the mass of society no longer have a place in the real post-sixties world.

It would be a mistake, though, to think that public relations practice in HE is just about succouring the finances of the college. It is not. A crucial element in the formulation of college PR strategy is recognising that *credibility is all* in the HE world. Why do students pick a particular college? Ask a few dozen, and you'll find that just about the most common answer is "because I've heard that it has a good reputation." The college that picks up a bad reputation − however unfounded it may be − sees its application levels plummet. Colleges that suddenly acquire a good press − as winners of *University Challenge* have often discovered − find on the contrary that they can sift through a particularly rich crop of applicants, and improved application levels mean the entrance of better-motivated, better-suited students, who in their turn will provide a continuing testimony to the college.

Other tangible assets of sound PR practice include: improved staff morale, with reduced turnover; more productive relationships with business, industry and the professions; more successful fund-raising activities; improved income levels from the conference, short-course, and full-cost course activities; and more beneficial relationships with local and national government and their officers. A really good public relations policy, supported by all levels of the college, can in fact be of major assistance in virtually all areas of the college's activity.

Such benefits usually lead the sceptics about college PR activity to admit that it has a point; the common fallback of such sceptics is then to assert that PR activity is something that their particular college cannot afford, because it is too small/too poor/too untroubled. They argue that their college does not, in its particular position, have sufficient cause to "have" public relations. As Roger Haywood points out, however,[2] "The decision is not whether to have public relations, but whether these relations will be handled in a planned, organised manner . . . or allowed to be accidental, haphazard, and possibly inconsistent." If the college is tiny, it can well be that the function of the PRP has to be taken on as one of a number of tasks of a senior member of staff. Most colleges with more than 2,000 full-time-equivalent students, however, have recognised that the job requires at least one member of staff committed full-time to it. The fact is that the college's PR profile is of *strategic* importance, not an optional extra.

What does the public relations practitioner actually do?
Since public relations is effected and affected by everyone within the college, the overarching responsibility for it must lie with the principal. No other person is in a better position to influence the actions and attitudes of colleagues, to require the following of procedures or to demand an explanation when things go wrong. No other person, from a public point of view, is better recognised as personifying the college; no other person is better placed to have an overall perspective of the best interests of the college. So what, then, is the role of the PRP?

Much public relations work is a matter of common sense, courtesy and sensitivity to others' reactions; some of it is the application of specialist techniques. A college that employs a trained and experienced PRP − whether on the staff or as a consultant − has the benefit of someone who, through the principal, can guide the adoption of a sound public relations policy, constantly assess or measure the state of the college's public relations, prepare a long-term public relations strategy, carry out specialist tasks, and encourage colleagues to inculcate a public relations outlook in the execution of their normal jobs.

PR often sounds to be a distinctly nebulous activity: some of the misgivings felt towards the profession are undoubtedly due to the assumption that PR officers proceed by arcane means, changing people's attitudes by some insidious process known only to the elect. We all fear and loathe the secret manipulators. In actual fact the day-to-day activities of the college PR office are far from nebulous, and far indeed from underhand. Perhaps the biggest contribution of PRPs is to prick their college in major and minor ways. They are often seen as the mouthpiece of their college, proclaiming its virtues and defending its transgressions, but in a real sense they are also the college's conscience. They are the outsider on the inside; the devil's advocate. They see the college as it really is, not as colleagues fondly imagine it to be. For this reason the presence on campus of a good PRP can be an uncomfortable experience for complacent colleagues.

PRPs should be constantly studying the world around them, holding up a finger for changes in the climate; they should assess the opportunities the changes might present, while advising how the college might avoid the dangers. They are monitors and prophets of external change and instigators of internal change. In addition to the role of advisor, PRPs will have a concrete daily workload of specialist tasks to execute. The mix of the daily routine will vary from college to college, but typically the jobs can include:

> Editing, designing, and arranging the printing, of prospectuses, leaflets, and other central publications; editing internal and alumni newsletters; writing and dispatching press releases and in other ways generating media interest in the college; dealing with media queries; encouraging the utilisation of college staff by the media; updating compendia; arranging exhibitions; overseeing visits to the college; speaking to schools, careers advisers and other groups; preparing material for fund-raising and income-generating activities; organising photographic sessions; preparing audio-visual material; helping address issues to policy makers; arranging awards and other ceremonies; controlling the college enquiries desk; conducting market and opinion surveys.

It has to be said that while the role of the PRP as described here is accepted in the more progressive industrial and commercial companies, its acceptance by colleges has not yet been widespread. More often the PRP − perhaps entitled "information officer" − is appointed with the expectation of carrying out some low-level tasks associated just with the dissemination of information by various means. He or she is often appointed at low salary, at a junior point of the college hierarchy, sometimes without appropriate training or experience, and often not allowed to affect policy in any way. That is not the kind of public relations that is covered by this book nor the kind that the authors advocate for any college that wants to face up realistically to present-day challenges. For those colleges that find themselves thinking of public relations solely as a "downstream" activity, perhaps the time has come for a re-assessment, and for placing their public relations function on a new, sound, footing.

Summary

Public relations activity is in no sense hostile to the college ideal, but an ethical endeavour wholly compatible with the pursuit, and dissemination, of truth. Public relations as treated in this book are something that no college can avoid having: relations with the public and with specific sections inevitably exist. If the relations are good they help the college enormously; if they are bad then they hinder everything the college tries to do. The PR climate can be improved by the adoption of certain principles and certain attitudes. It is the duty of the college principal to ensure that the college operates in as favourable a climate as possible. While it is proper for principals to execute major public relations roles themselves they are likely to perform these roles more effectively if the college employs a good PRP; there are also many straightforward day-to-day functions performed by the PRP which support the work of the college in diverse ways, none of which involve arcane, or secretly manipulative, procedures.

Chapter 2. Clarifying the Goals

Introduction

In the 1970s, when electronic data processing still seemed new and exotic, many a company decided that it was time to buy itself a computer. Often, the main reasons were:

(1) that was what their main competitors were doing;
(2) computerisation was obviously the way forward for any get-ahead company.

Managements often failed to ask the basic question: "what exactly do we want a computer to do?" It is not surprising that over half of the first-time buyers in the 1970s gained no real benefits from the acquisition. It often seems that "setting up a PR office" in the 1980s is set to follow a similar pattern.

There are of course some excellent reasons for buying computers; similarly there are excellent reasons for establishing a public relations office. Amongst these, however, are not the vague feeling that a PRP will act as a magic charm to keep the UGC[3] or NAB[4] sweet and ward off evil newspaper reports. If a public relations office is to achieve results, it won't be due to arcane activities hidden far from the mainstream of college work. Worthwhile achievements only come about if a public relations programme becomes an integral element of the college's management scheme, with clear, agreed goals based on a true understanding of the PR realities, and a means of measuring whether targets are met.

In the absence of a sound understanding of the PR realities, sensible programmes and targets are unlikely to be formulated. In the absence of programmes and targets, PRPs can only guess where their priorities should lie. In the absence of measured achievements, management cannot be reassured that their money is being spent to any purpose.

Research

Sound planning, of course, has to be based on solid information, as is recognised in all spheres of activity: most areas of work seem to have an adage equivalent to the military's "time spent on reconnaissance is never wasted". Acquiring and analysing "hard" facts, such as data on demographic trends, is known to be a primary need of sound management, but quite as important is gaining an understanding of apparently "soft" information: the attitudes and beliefs of the people relevant to the organisation's success. Businesses have learnt the tough way that they must gain sound "intelligence" if they are to prosper, and substantial sums are now spent on research into markets, attitudes and opinions before new products are developed and launched. Sir Clive Sinclair's failure to conduct such research properly before embarking on his ill-fated electric vehicle programme provided one of the most vivid recent illustrations of why the research is essential.

Most of us tend to suppose that our antennae are well-attuned to other people's beliefs and behaviour, and yet it is very dangerous to base our plans on personal hunches, or on generalisations from the reactions of acquaintances. It would clearly be wasteful, for instance, for a company to spend large sums on an advertising campaign to correct a supposed misperception, if the company was not sure that the misperception was widely held by people who mattered to the company's success. Even if a survey simply confirms a hunch, quantification enables the issue to be taken seriously, while providing a base point against which the success of subsequent programmes can be measured.

When an organisation knows, through careful information-gathering, what its public relations problems are, then it can construct public relations programmes which can tackle the real issues head on. If a polytechnic knows, for example, that 65% of the local population do not recognise that it teaches degree courses, then a structured programme can be created to help deal with the misperception: booklets and leaflets can be prepared for the local community explaining the degree course offerings; the weekly article written for the main local paper can always refer to one or other of the degree courses; stories about successful local degree students can be released regularly to the local media; local advertisements and talks to local groups can stress the degrees, and so forth. To give another example, if research indicates that a particular university is disliked because it is thought to accept only the children of the rich, then a programme can be devised to demonstrate the various ways in which the university ensures substantial intakes from a wide cross-section of the community.

Surveys of the key audiences will always provide material suggesting the need for PR programmes, and will give essential information in deciding the priority to be given to each element of the programme. Knowledge of the audiences also allows practice of management by anticipation rather than by crisis. There might, for instance, be a serious problem building up with a particular audience, which − in the absence of research to bring it to light − will only be recognised when a storm has broken: when the students' association has occupied the administrative centre; when planning permission for a major building is turned down because of neighbours' hostility; when an animal rights group has smashed thousands of pounds worth of equipment. Advance knowledge of a problem can very often lead to a cessation of hostilities before battle lines are formed.

Academic institutions pride themselves on being the home of sound research, and clearly owe it to themselves not to be amateurish in the quality of research into matters affecting their operational success. It is pleasing, therefore, that colleges do indeed conduct fairly regular research into their main "market": potential students. Surveys of the motivation of new students are fairly commonplace, providing information on the relative importance of different elements of a college's promotional activities. Most colleges also, at some time or another, study their patterns of recruitment in order to understand where promotional efforts can be most effectively centred.

Sadly, however, there is at present very little systematic research into broader college PR issues, and particularly into the perceptions of higher education as a whole and its three main constituent parts: colleges of HE, polytechnics, and universities. A huge number of questions always arise whenever an individual PRP sets about formulating public relations programmes. A few examples should make this clear. Is quality control through external validation, which is felt to be a great strength of polytechnics by those who understand its workings, perceived in fact by careers advisers as a serious weakness, because it implies that polytechnics can't look after themselves? Is the resentment felt towards higher education amongst some social groups, resulting from its restrictions on entry, of greater moment than the respect felt in those groups for the high entry standards? Is development of access perceived by various publics as socially and economically beneficial, or viewed rather as a dilution of standards? Would a "small is beautiful" campaign help the colleges and institutes of higher education, or is there an inevitable association of size with strength? Does the general public recognise a distinction between further education colleges and polytechnics? Are student marches, which certainly aid public recognition of the problems of HE, nevertheless counter-productive overall, owing to the hostility caused?

Views on dozens of issues such as these need to be formed by PRPs, as they will radically affect the purposes of PR programmes and the techniques used. Often, views will have to be formed on limited evidence. Only rarely, at present, does solid evidence become available – the famous MORI poll[5] of 1983/4 into the perceptions of polytechnics was influential precisely because such data is produced so rarely. It is to be hoped that higher education, a business with a total turnover of several billion pounds a year, will, in fact, soon come to support such centralised information-gathering on a regular basis. Meanwhile, individual colleges and PRPs will need to gather as much information as possible on their own. Research can be a highly skilled business, but is not necessarily expensive. Quite small pilot studies can provide sufficient information on which to base a programme. Since solid information is something of which organisations are always short, however, it would be wise to include at least one thorough survey in the PR programme each year. Many colleges have departments of business studies in which the techniques of opinion and market research are studied. It would be quite proper to ask such departments to carry out research on perceptions of their own institution, and would give students an actual rather than theoretical problem on which to work while minimising costs to the institution.

Aims, goals, objectives
Throughout this book it will be stressed constantly that public relations practice *must* have aims and objectives. The scarcest resource in any public relations programme is the human resource. Typically public relations staffs are small, and their workload is high: no matter how much work is done, there is always *more* waiting to be done. Effort should therefore never be expended "just on PR", but must always be applied for clearly known purposes.

All PRPs must certainly be fully aware of the overall purposes of their work if it is to be effective. When challenged to describe their jobs it has been known for some college PRPs to say "to provide information" – and yet there is little point in providing information unless it is done for a purpose. The underlying purpose on one occasion might be to encourage school-leavers to apply to the college; on another, it might be to influence people to think well of the college; on a third occasion it might be to pre-empt an unfavourable press report. The information-dissemination process will always be more productive, however, if PRPs grasp not just the immediate purposes of an activity, but the overall purposes of their work: irrelevances will be omitted, key factors stressed, appropriate examples used, the right audiences reached, and a suitable amount of effort will be put into each activity.

A college employing public relations staff must similarly have a clear view of why it is making the appointment(s). It may not be possible, it is true, to lay down detailed objectives at the pre-appointment stage, because when professional people are being brought in, it can be an advantage to allow their expertise, once in post, to determine the setting of detailed objectives. Nevertheless some broad public relations goals can be identified which, if achieved, will help the college to pursue more easily its functions of educating students and engaging in scholarship.

Definitions

In management theory "aims", "goals" and "objectives" are terms which are scattered around liberally. Sometimes they are used interchangeably, and one book often contradicts another on definitions. The co-authors will try to avoid confusion by using the terms in the following ways:

Aims — the fundamental purposes for which the college was established. These are often given in founding documents such as charters, and may refer for example to teacher training, undergraduate teaching, adult education, or research, perhaps stressing a particular approach to them.

Goals — the long-range and medium-range targets that lie ahead of management action programmes. They are stated in the college's regular planning papers, and might be, for example, to put up new buildings; to increase the proportion of women students; to merge with another college; to collaborate with industry in offering more relevant courses, etc.

Objectives — the specific results that are required to be achieved in a given time scale. They follow from the aims and goals and are supportive of them: e.g. to have 150 electrical engineering trainees three years from now; to be recognised by an extra 5% of the local population in each of the next four years; to reduce the fuel bill by 10% next year; to be visited by the local MP or the Lord Mayor at least once this year.

Setting goals

An ongoing question for employers of college PRPs, and the PRPs themselves, must be "what specific goals does the college need to achieve through a public relations programme, and in what order of priority?" The answers, of course, will differ from college to college, and from time to time, as conditions and aspirations vary. Some will want above all else to throw off a negative and damaging reputation; others will see the main need as obtaining a fairer share of the financial cake; yet others will see the first priority as attracting staff and students of the very highest order. There should always be the clearest lines of communication between the principal and the PRP on any special features of the college's goals: it would be ridiculous, for example, for the principal to formulate the goal of increasing the proportion of women and minority-group students in the college, and yet not to make this plain to the PRP, whose work can have a major impact on its delivery.

Chapter 6 will discuss the issue of how colleges can plan their specific programmes, working out a system of priorities given the resources available. The next chapter, however, will discuss seven particular goals of public relations programmes, as these are shared by virtually all colleges in the UK.

Summary
Appointment of a public relations practitioner should be based on clear views about its purpose. The appointment by itself will not cure ills or produce magic results, but must be a tangible recognition of the fact that public relations goals have been identified and that the PRP will have the college's support in trying to achieve them. PRPs will need to agree with their employers the objectives of their work programme, based on sound research into the views of the college's publics. Similarly, objectives need to be quantified, so that the PRP and the employers can check whether over time the objectives have been met. These objectives must follow from, and support, the fundamental aims of the college and its current goals.

Chapter 3. Seven Specific Goals

Though the number of possible PR goals of colleges is enormous, since each is in various ways unique, there are a small number of PR issues common to all institutions of higher education. This chapter will discuss seven of the most common goals of college PR, considering various lines of attack and offering suggestions as to how achievements with respect to them can be measured.

1. Increasing the level of suitably qualified, suitably motivated, applicants.

This is the bread-and-butter work of most college PRPs, since in the absence of sufficient students, a great deal of money is lost (several thousand pounds a year for each degree student below capacity) while in the absence of students of the right quality, staff and student morale declines along with the college reputation. There are many promising lines of attack — but research is vital in planning the campaign.

It soon becomes clear, in fact, that attraction of students is one of the points at which public relations and marketing converge, many of the techniques of the latter becoming highly relevant. Views will have to be formed about what factors influence potential applicants and their advisers — and this involves market research. Well-founded judgements will have to be made on what weight should be attached to improving the prospectus and other central publications; on the proportion of effort to be put into schools and careers officer liaison; on the relative cost-effectiveness of various forms of advertising; on the importance of media coverage to application levels; and on the place and importance of consumer guides and compendia.

Concentrating on effective methods of publicity, however, should not blind the college to the need for the other main public relations function: to monitor closely what potential applicants think of the college. For colleges which recruit mainly at school-leaving age, the schools liaison programmes should pay particular attention to obtaining this kind of feedback. Do the school pupils think highly of the college? Do they have a prejudice against it? Are they misinformed? Have they, in fact, discerned genuine faults in the college?

Once an initial decision is made on distribution of personnel and cash resources, a system for measuring success or failure needs to be devised. Changes in gross application levels are sometimes considered sufficiently informative, but a far better indicator may be market share, readily deducible by universities and polytechnics through a study of UCCA[6] and PCAS[7] statistics. Some means of checking quality is also necessary: many thousands of unsuitable applicants can be a time-wasting inconvenience: what are really needed are appropriately qualified and appropriately motivated applications. A-level scores of ultimate entrants compared to those of other colleges are thus often treated as more significant than gross application levels, and certainly provide some indication of the relative attractiveness of colleges and departments – or the effectiveness of their promotional activity. Another useful set of figures indicating relative attractiveness are the ratios of offers made to students enrolled; reduction of these ratios can provide a particularly useful quantified objective.

High gross numbers of applicants should not be too readily dismissed as wasteful, though. In one sense a high application rate is a useful indicator of the popularity of the college: over time a valuable trend can be plotted. Also, all the people who take the trouble to apply are showing that they think reasonably well of the college, particularly if they use up one of their valuable UCCA[8] or PCAS[9] choices. Even if many of them do not become students they are still potential supporters of the college in the future. In handling their applications, therefore, there is an opportunity to build goodwill amongst a significant sector of society. At the time of writing, for instance, some twenty-five thousand people per year are applying for Oxford Polytechnic courses, while only about 1200 will gain places: it would be a foolish step indeed to turn the initial interest of such large numbers of people into resentment.

Over-application might, in the absence of a PR perspective, be regarded as an administrative inconvenience, handled by a curtly worded rejection letter; alternatively, it can be treated as a public relations opportunity to be handled sensitively with thanks, regret, good wishes and positive advice. In the case of the Open University, applications for its undergraduate courses have always exceeded the number of places available. Although the OU hates to turn away many thousands of applicants each year it has introduced a policy of guaranteeing entry for the following year. It has also recognised that the continuing high demand has beneficially affected the Government's financial policy towards it.

2. Helping the college become better known.

> I don't know you or your company. I have never heard of your products. In my eyes you have no track record. Your reputation is non-existent, whilst your competitors are reputable, well-established, familiar and know how to work with my company . . . . Now, what are you trying to sell me?[10]

Some colleges are felt to be "a part of the scene" because they are so often referred to in speeches at conferences and elsewhere and so often appear in some shape or form in media coverage; others (usually those with no organised PR effort) are rarely if ever heard about, and thus just *don't seem to count*. It is a well-documented fact[11] that the better known an organisation, the more we feel able to deal with it with confidence. If a new product is launched by a well-known firm such as ICI or Marks & Spencer then we as consumers are more likely to buy it than if a similar product is launched by a firm with an unfamiliar name. Enlightened managements in higher education, certainly, will realise that barely known colleges are likely to be losing out on applicants and credibility, and won't be able to call on many friends when the going gets tough. It is a classic situation calling for PR expertise − rather more so than the situation of bolstering application levels, which needs a judicious mix of marketing with the PR practitioner's own special skills.

Most items in the armamentarium of the PR office, in fact, come into play when the goal is squarely to put the college on the map. First, target audiences are identified and an attempt is made to find out what if any are their views on the college. Decisions are then made on which of the audiences will respond most readily and beneficially to attention and what media or other mechanisms will be effective in reaching those audiences. Press statements begin to flow, supported by various other techniques: anything from leaflet campaigns to paid advertising, from open days to slide shows and videos, from exhibitions to radio phone-ins.

Measurement of such efforts tends to focus on opinion surveys, conversations with selected individuals, and analyses of press cuttings over a set period. Results are nearly always encouraging when comparing the period before and after a new PR programme. From a base of zero effort much can be achieved with the first few steps. Far less encouraging will be the results of comparison surveys, and comparison press-cutting analyses, where the comparator is a college known to have a better-resourced public relations office staffed by people of talent. Such comparisons, indeed, can be deeply chastening. After all, public relations is more effective as a long-term policy. True results are likely to be established only after two or three years of continuous effort.

3. Helping the college gain an enhanced reputation

This might seem to be the same objective as that of section 2. So far as colleges are concerned, most news *is* good news, and anything which helps a college become better known will also tend to increase the esteem in which it held. Worcester's Law[12] also tells us that familiarity breeds favourability, rather than contempt. This is not, however, invariably so, as the Polytechnic of North London found out in 1984,[13] and several universities discovered to their cost in the days of student militancy. Not a few colleges, indeed, have a specific need to replace a negative reputation caused by being too well known for the wrong reasons. This is a situation requiring more carefully targeted PR procedures. Usually, the approach is to implement a campaign focusing on a few specific strengths, with the goal of associating the college in the minds of the general public primarily with those areas of strength, rather than the previous area of weakness. This issue, which is closely tied in with the concept of projecting a corporate identity, is discussed further in Chapter 10.

Two principles

Two principles need to be stated at this stage.

First, in the long run no college can obtain a good reputation unless it deserves to have one. Some commentators view a PRP as someone who gives a rosy appearance to something that is less than good. The PRP, however, must be concerned equally with substance and appearance. If the college is worthwhile – good academic standards, pastoral concern for its students, sound research and so on – then the PRP can deploy techniques to ensure that the college's worth becomes fully appreciated. If it is found that the college is lacking in quality, however, then the PRP's first task is to bring the faults to the attention of the principal, other senior staff, or appropriate committees, for action to be taken. If the college has a wide reputation for weak research, for instance, and this is damaging the credibility of everything it does, then the PRP must explain the fact carefully, and see that action is taken to overcome the deficiency. Faults such as this might be taken for granted as unchangeable by academics and administrators who have been in post for some time, or they might not even be noticed by those who have never known anything different. PRPs, on the other hand, using their "outsider" vision, and the results of opinion surveys, can clearly pinpoint the failings. Only when the failings have been corrected can there be a reality of which an image is worth projecting.

The second principle is that quality does not necessarily speak for itself. There are some academics who shy away from the adoption of a public relations policy because they feel it is unnecessary. They have a view that if a college gets on with its job of producing good students and good scholarship its worth will become obvious. Realistically, though, in today's fast-moving, highly communicative world, the Bible's "by their fruits ye shall know them" has to be coupled with the American aphorism "it's no use having a good trumpet unless you blow it."

Good works and quality do, indeed, become known but the pace of recognition is often very slow. In some cases individuals have long been dead before history books have chronicled their merit for the first time. A college can rarely afford to wait for generations in order to establish a good reputation. In some circumstances it might be forced into extinction before the paymasters have realised its worth.

4. Influencing decision-makers to smile upon one's college

This area of public relations has probably received more conscious attention than any other since 1981, when the big cuts took place. Colleges have always tried to influence their paymasters, of course, but until the great swings of Sir Keith Joseph's axe[14] those efforts were rather more concealed; it was no doubt considered unseemly to be obvious about the attempt to influence. That activity, nevertheless, is one of the stones on which democratic structures are founded. MPs and local councillors are elected to carry out the wishes of the people. In turn, ministers, education committees and governing bodies are appointed or elected to turn those wishes into policies. How can they know what the wishes of the people are unless they are articulated?

In Britain the word "lobbying" is regarded with suspicion, but lobbying in all its forms is widely practised. Its activities fall into two broad categories: direct and indirect. Direct lobbying involves communicating in person with the decision-makers and their immediate associates, whether face-to-face, in a letter, or by telephone. Indirect lobbying involves the use of channels of communication which are known to reach the decision-makers ultimately, even though the message passes through third party hands initially and may be made available to many other people en route. To a certain extent, media relations bear the brunt of such efforts: politicians and others in public office usually pay careful attention to the media coverage relevant to their various constituents, and well-placed press stories can pay off handsomely.[15] Often the only amendment to normal media-liaison procedures is to ensure that particular attention is paid to the specific media most used by the decision makers. If the main targets are local politicians, then local papers are covered most carefully; if the main targets are national politicians, efforts are channelled rather more to the quality dailies; if the main targets are members of the University Grants Committee or Council for National Academic Awards, then the *Times Higher Education Supplement* becomes a particularly important publication.

However, indirect lobbying is not *confined* to media relations. Decision makers are, like all of us, individual members of society. They move in social and business circles and their thinking is affected by the views that are expressed by other people in those circles. Endorsement of one's case by a third-party acquaintance of a decision-maker can often be more effective than any presentation by oneself. Hence, talks to Rotary Clubs or Townswomen's Guilds, for example, or campus visits by influential businessmen, or student fund-raising for hospitals and other charities, might all have a political impact beyond the original purpose of each event. Clearly, however, care must be taken not to put too much effort into such activities if indirect lobbying − which may or may not be achieved − is the main intention. A proper balance has to be kept between direct and indirect lobbying.

Visits to the college, usually including lunches or dinner, also tend to play a significant role in dealings with decision-makers, and not simply because of the view that anyone who has eaten at our table is less likely to be mean to us. At least as significant is the fact that if one's college is to the foreground, rather than background, of the visitor's consciousness, then the college's concerns are more likely to be taken seriously. Any well-prepared visit allows great scope for the public relations practitioner: through carefully prepared presentations, exhibitions, slide shows, and special visit publications, a great deal of relevant information can be conveyed to the visitor very quickly, and both the information, and the professionalism with which it is conveyed, can increase the respect in which the college is held.

Lobbying is one of those areas with which the PRP is expected to have great expertise. Whenever cut-backs are threatened, in fact, the main cry from senior committees can be to "lobby the politicians". It is not always clear exactly what is expected; perhaps it is assumed that it is only at this stage that "PR" is necessary, and that since PR is all about the hocus-pocus of opinion-manipulating, committee members shouldn't be expected to soil their hands with the messy details. In the experience of many college PRPs, however, instant lobbying is grossly overemphasised by senior committees, carrying with it wholly unreasonable expectations. Attempting to bend the ear of strangers when you are in difficulties, and when you've never previously attempted to address them, can sometimes be counter-productive. We have all heard stories of the individual who snatches defeat from the jaws of victory through attempts at ingratiating or brow-beating politicians. Real success in public relations does not come in this manner, but by the steady, year-after-year business of careful communication.

The college that regularly invites its MP to events; that keeps the MP informed of the successes of staff and students; that courteously takes an interest in the MP's own successes: it is this college which justifiably feels it has a right to speak to the MP when times are suddenly hard. Successful lobbying is in fact rarely more than a matter of calling on influential friends when they are needed — and first, you have to get yourself the influential friends.

Measuring the success of some lobbying activities can be very easy. If, for instance, a college wants to obtain some concession from its decision-makers then the objective can be seen to have been achieved or not according to whether or not the concession was granted. Other successes or failures might have to be measured subjectively. Has the college's case been adequately presented by a third party? Were its research activities mentioned in a particular parliamentary debate? Were its achievements mentioned in the local authority annual report?

For regular and accurate tracking of top attitudes towards the college, professional firms can be used to carry out opinion research. This is the most reliable method but it is likely to prove too expensive for many colleges. In these circumstances it is well to remember the two-way function of public relations. Every time contact is made with important people the college should listen as well as talk. The desire to impart information about the college, its plight and its good works, should not outweigh the need to give VIPs time to indicate their own attitudes; indeed they should be gently questioned on whether they have any reservations about the college's case or whether they support it.

5. Improving internal relations
The value of sound internal relations is hard to overestimate. For one thing, the college's staff and students represent potential ambassadors numbered by the thousand. If this army understands, and identifies with, the problems and aspirations of the college, then issues of external relations can be dealt with on a scale far beyond that of any single public relations practitioner. Nevertheless, this is not the main point of sound internal relations. Just as external relations has regard for the public interest, so internal relations is based on genuine consideration for the human capital that the college employs and for the students it teaches.

The staff have a genuine stake in their college; their employment is not simply a matter of exchanging money for their services. They spend a third of their waking hours in the college for many years of their lives. They are individuals with the full array of emotions, ambitions, desires and physical abilities. Good internal relations pays attention to them as people. It acknowledges that working for the college can be, for them, either a mindless, mechanical chore or a genuine contribution to their enjoyment of life.

One vital element of internal relations is good communications. People like to know where they fit into an organisation: they cannot see this unless they are kept informed about the organisation, its plans, its successes, its problems. They need to know that their worries and concerns are recognised by colleagues and senior management.

But good or bad internal communications can have other effects for the organisation. During the 1970s numerous managements in the industrial world found to their horror that failure to communicate with the internal audience was putting the entire organisation in peril. Often enough, reluctance to enact a programme of communication meant that unions monopolised this function, with the result that every management decision was second-guessed, and management credibility was undermined. Trainee managers are now taught that the result of leaving information dispersal to others or the grapevine is wholly unnecessary conflict with employees, making achievement of the organisation's goals far more difficult. Of course this isn't simply a lesson learned from industrial conflicts in the 1970s. The main theme of Plato's *Republic* revolved around the point that any organisation which is internally harmonious, with all its parts co-operating towards a common goal, can achieve results far in excess of those organisations divided against themselves.

Work on newsletters, noticeboards, electronic noticeboards, and internal exhibitions, are amongst the specific duties of a sound college PR office. These will significantly supplement, though not replace, the commitment of the leadership to open management and wide consultation. Without such a commitment to open management, in fact, the PRP's efforts are likely to be wasted, being perceived by staff and students as nothing more than an attempt by "the management" to fob them off with superficiality, skirting around the real issues.

If a house journal is introduced then a number of policy matters have to be determined at the outset. These policies will guide editors in their choice of content, the format (magazine or newspaper), the language used, and the frequency of publication.

First, what is the purpose of the journal? Is it intended as a one-way communication for purveying "official" views, or is it genuinely a two-way means of communication? If it is the latter then there has to be a liberal editorial policy. There can be no real censorship, or it will lose its credibility. Sensitive issues will have to be covered, controversial viewpoints reported, and readers' letters criticising management published.

Second, who is it produced for — staff or students or both? If it is for staff, then is it for all staff or just for academics and professional administrators? A journal for all staff must recognise that all readers do not have background knowledge such as access to committee papers, so issues will have to be explained from scratch. The language used must be equally intelligible to gardeners, secretaries, and academics alike.

Third, is it designed only for an on-campus audience or is it intended also for external readership? If the latter, then many compromises will be necessary, which will prevent successful communications with either audience. It might seem wasteful to produce two separate journals which would often cover similar topics, but a single journal which is read by neither audience would be very much more wasteful.

The effectiveness of some elements of internal communications can be assessed fairly easily by surveys which check the degree of staff and student knowledge about current issues and key figures before and after a programme has been put into effect. The surveys need not be elaborate ones, carried out by professional firms. Much useful feedback can be obtained by an inexpensive, home-produced but carefully structured questionnaire or set of interviews. The extent of ignorance discovered, both before the programme and after it has been working for some time, will be distressing — but clear improvements should at least be registered and will show why efforts to enhance internal communications are essential. Levels of apathy and motivation are rather harder to measure, but a useful approach is to include, in the questionnaires on which the surveys are based, statements of the college's policy along with the question *"do you agree/disagree"*, giving a scale of the level. Employees like to think that their views are being noted and can be of influence, and thus tend to co-operate well with such surveys. Policies of open management, combined with college-wide consultation and attention to techniques of internal communication, should over time register dramatic increases in the level of concurrence between the views of the staff and the senior management.

6. Maintaining good relations with the community
It is important for all colleges to be recognised as worthy members of the local community, though the fact has often been obvious only to those in what was once known as "Local Authority Higher Education", then "Public Sector Higher Education", and now, it seems, the "Polytechnic and College Sector of Higher Education" (PCSHE). Such col-

leges had become only too aware of the financial power of local councillors in administering the "topping up" grant and the college's capital expenditure. Local councillors have also played a leading role on college governing bodies, and the local authority, again, has acted as intermediary in many of the colleges' dealings with national bodies. Relationships with the local community have thus been ignored at the PCSHE college's peril: if the college neighbours had resented its presence, wholehearted support for the college from their elected representatives would not have been forthcoming.

A number of PCSHE colleges, recognising all this, have put considerable effort into ensuring that an understanding of the college is transmitted to the local community, through techniques such as development of relationships with the local media, leafleting campaigns, open days, provision of speakers for local groups, participation in community projects, and booklets aimed directly at the region. Care has usually been taken to explain to the ratepayers that the college is far from a drain on their purse, being funded essentially from national funds while making a major contribution to the local economy. The average polytechnic, for instance, has been able to point out that it injects, directly or indirectly, over 20 million pounds into the local economy, and provides over one thousand local jobs.

If the local authorities' control over PCSHE colleges were to wane,[16] motivation to maintain good links would be reduced. Even colleges which are subject to few controls by the local authority are nevertheless unwise to neglect local sensibilities. The local authority will still retain power to approve or obstruct building plans, and they — like all members of the local community — remain an easily accessible audience on which messages will have a significant impact. And different audiences talk to one another. Immediate neighbours talk to others in the region, and to MPs and the papers, and if they don't like the college, they — whose opinions gain credibility by the fact that they can see the college's washing on the line, clean or dirty — can do a great deal of harm. Often enough, immediate neighbours have perfectly fair criticisms: students taking short-cuts through their property; noise from late-night dances; over-enthusiastic revelry after final exams; traffic problems. The objections need to be listened to. If the neighbours realise that the college will listen, and act where possible on their complaints, much of the antagonism dissipates. Goodwill can be fostered, too, if the immediate neighbours are kept informed of college activities that might be of interest, and encouraged to use facilities such as libraries, squash courts, the catering management training restaurant, or careers centres. Councillors and MPs, who have not just the college, but its neighbours, as constituents, will be a lot more supportive if that college has a reputation as a caring member of the community.

Beyond self-interest there is a further reason why colleges should establish good community relations. By definition, a worthwhile college is a centre of excellence. Its staff comprise a group of experts who are being salaried by public funds. Is it too altruistic to suggest that every community where a college is located should feel the benefits of the expertise that is in their midst? The economic and social problems of the area should receive extra attention. The quality of life should feel enriched. In short, the civic pride that went into founding the red-brick universities and "techs" a century ago should be in evidence today.

7. Maintaining productive relations with alumni.

Marketeers pay careful attention to recent customers, with very good reason: such individuals have proven themselves to be "in the market", and thus likely either to buy again, or at least to influence others to make a similar purchase. Until recently most colleges in Britain seemed to think this element of the marketing approach irrelevant to higher education, but they were thereby missing an important trick. While it may be true that only a small proportion of graduates "buy again" by returning to their old college for some form of continuing professional development, they can certainly be of great influence in generating potential applicants, and creating a favourable climate of opinion about a college. Where overseas students are concerned, indeed, it is known that the returned student is one of the chief sources of further recruitment.

The main importance of alumni, though, lies outside the "sales" area. For most colleges, their existence was largely overlooked until the hard years; then, attention turned first to their potential as coffer-fillers, and secondly, to their potential as voters and writers of letters to MPs.

The approach of American universities to alumni relations, which has generated extremely impressive sums of money on a continuing basis — now over a billion dollars a year in total — led their British counterparts in the early eighties to take alumni bank balances very seriously. It soon became apparent, though, that British alumni have rather different calls on their wallets from their U.S. equivalent. American graduates, for one thing, have a greater disposable income, and this allows them to be much more amenable to calls for contributions, particularly since such calls are an acknowledged part of American culture. The British experience to date, therefore, has been that only those colleges which attract unusually well-heeled students can expect financial success in this area to come easily: others certainly *can* raise funds, but the proportion of money raised to effort expended often discourages further initiatives. Rather than attempting to raise funds on a continuing basis, many have been contenting themselves just with occasional fund-raising drives, though some universities have taken a longer-term view and have been developing mechanisms for achieving more ambitious targets. Colleges are wise in attempting to change the culture towards alumni contribution, rather than accepting that nothing can change, but it will take much effort indeed before American levels of success become commonplace.

All colleges, nevertheless, can score significantly in the "friend raising" stakes. It is a cliché, but nonetheless true, that many students will have spent the happiest years of their lives at college, making at that stage personal friends for life: it is not at all difficult, as a result, for the college to maintain their continued interest. A relatively inexpensive programme of keeping in touch, involving maintenance of addresses and distribution of yearly or twice-yearly newsletters, can be surprisingly well received. Alumni like to hear news about the *alma mater*. Even a digest of the year's internal newsletters, with a sprinkling of news about long-standing college personalities and interesting alumni, can be remarkably well received, generating a number of letters.

No college can have too many friends, and alumni can be very good friends indeed. A small minority, for example, can be cultivated to act as local representatives, performing functions such as addressing schools about college life, contacting employers about industrial placements, ensuring that college consultancy services are recognised, or even pushing the college's conference and holiday facilities. A larger number will show themselves willing to return to the college to give careers advice. A larger number still will prove themselves willing to provide verbal support for college causes so long as the college takes the trouble to keep in regular contact with them and provides the stimulus.

Ensuring that communications are two-way, and keeping tabs on what alumni are accomplishing, can also provide information invaluable for other areas of public relations: it is the college's products, after all, which must be its ultimate testimony. Oxford Polytechnic, for instance, has found it productive on various occasions to point out that the world's most successful exporter of racing cars started off by assembling a prototype racing car as a final-year project in his Oxford Polytechnic engineering course. This one example speaks more eloquently about the value of the project system – and of the engineering course it was part of – than a thousand pages of validators' documentation. Other institutions, of course, can trump this by listing prime ministers, members of the cabinet, or Nobel prize winners, who were given the first impetus to their future careers during their college days.

If alumni are an active ingredient of a college community then that institution is immeasurably stronger in society. As the number of graduates grows with the passing of years, even the silent majority can become useful allies of the college. Quite small colleges can often number their graduates in tens of thousands: and graduates inevitably become more influential than the average citizen. Though an individual alumnus may give only very limited support to the alma mater, even when prodded, the combined overall effect of such a supporters' club can be of great importance. It should also be remembered that there is now a total of over 2 million graduates in the country, each of them receptive to messages from their old college. Had that army of influential graduates been kept in close touch with college events in the late seventies and early eighties, it is quite likely that the recent history of higher education would have been far less troublesome.

Summary

Amongst the common PR goals of colleges are: to increase the number of suitable applicants; to become better known; to enhance the college reputation; to influence decision-makers; to improve internal relations; to enjoy good relations with the community; and to benefit from productive relationships with alumni. Public relations activity should be seen, throughout, as a two-way function, involving listening as well as informing. It also involves work whose effect can, and should, be measured.

Chapter 4. The Audiences

The last two chapters have stressed the importance of establishing goals and objectives. In public relations terms these goals are usually concerned with influencing – by fair and open methods – the attitudes, opinions and actions of people or groups of people and of monitoring their views about the college. In the jargon these people are known as "target audiences". The metaphor of the target is appropriate because it implies that careful aiming is needed to reach any particular audience. People differ in interests and receptiveness, so a method that is suitable for reaching one section of society may be wholly ineffective in reaching another.

For each goal it is possible to identify specific audiences. If the goal is to increase the number of applicants to a college, the most important target audiences are likely to be sixth-form pupils, head teachers, careers advisers, careers teachers, parents, and local authority careers officers. If the goal is to improve internal relations, the target audiences will be the various groups of staff and students: senior academics, junior academics, administrators, secretaries, clerks, technicians, manual staff, student officers, full-time students (residential and non-residential), part-time students, etc.

It will already be clear that if one were to itemise all possible college public relations goals, and then for each goal to itemise all the target audiences, divided into relevant sub-categories, the list of audiences would be very long indeed. Even when sub-classifications are ignored, the list would be extensive. It is, nevertheless, worth enumerating the key audiences of college PR: the list that *ought* to appear in virtually all colleges' plans. This is as follows — note, however, that it is not as yet in any order of priority.

Key target audiences
1 Primary decision-makers in national government and related national organisations (front-benchers, senior civil servants, quango chairmen, etc)
2 Secondary decision-makers in national government and related national organisations (back-benchers, opposition MPs, peers, junior civil servants, etc)
3 Holders of the main purse (NAB/PCFC, WAB, UGC/UFC, DES, etc)
4 Decision-makers in local government
5 Present students and staff
6 Potential staff
7 Potential students
8 The advisers of potential students
9 Ex-students and ex-staff
10 The local voter/ratepayer
11 The national voter/taxpayer
12 The college's neighbours
13 The research councils
14 Potential employers of graduates
15 Industry, commerce and the professions
16 Pressure groups relevant to education
17 Representative bodies (CVCP, CDP, SCOP, AUT, NATFHE, APT, etc)

The size of even this, comparatively limited, list makes it obvious that there are so many potential audiences for PR activity that a means of deciding their relative importance is essential if PR time and money is to be used to best effect. The last two chapters began the process of helping prioritise goals; this chapter will help with the process of prioritising audiences. As a result, it will be possible to move on with greater confidence to the prioritisation of activities, allowing a more objective view to be taken about how much time and effort should be put into each area of work.   The co-authors have developed independently a number of theoretical frameworks which they have found helpful when trying to set priorities in their own programmes of work; some are given in this chapter, and others are expounded more fully in Chapter 6 and Appendix 4. Although the frameworks are sometimes expressed in mathematical terms, it is recognised of course that public relations cannot be reduced to a set of mathematical expressions, any more than can the work of the personnel officer or lawyer. Nevertheless, the techniques outlined can allow the PRP to move far beyond the stage of acting on hunches: they allow clarification of assumptions, and previously unconscious thought-processes to be articulated and examined. Readers who are not PRPs might nevertheless prefer to obtain a general impression of the approaches outlined through mathematical formulae rather than follow the explanations in detail.

Prioritising audiences, method 1 – the goodwill test

A useful first step in estimating the relative importance of audiences is to ask how dependent is the college on their goodwill.[17] Is an audience's goodwill (a) crucial to the college's day-to-day existence; (b) essential to its long-term health; (c) desirable and clearly efficacious; (d) desirable but not clearly efficacious?

A test for this categorisation comes from asking of a target audience what is the impact on the college of the audience's support (or lack of it) for the college's goals. Let us consider first the existing staff and students. It should be evident that if they substantially reject the goals of the college, then that college can just no longer operate; it cannot continue effectively on a day-to-day basis. Existing staff and students, therefore, are in category (a): crucial to the college's day-to-day existence. Consider, next, the ex-staff. It would certainly be desirable for ex-staff to continue to support the college's goals: it is nice to see ex-colleagues again when they visit, and their support just might be valuable, for example by giving advice, by acting on friends-of-the-college committees, by making supportive comments in the community, or even through mentions in the will! Ex-staff, nevertheless, would in general only be in category (d): desirable but not clearly efficacious.

Examples of categories (b) and (c) can be found by considering the research councils and the holders of the main purse. For virtually all colleges, it counts as more than simply "nice" if members of research councils are supportive of the college and its goals. Good hard cash, in significant quantities, is involved; cash without which the college could, indeed, survive – but less happily. The research councils, therefore, can be classified as in category (c), as desirable and clearly efficacious. The holders of the main college purse, however, are even more important. If they (the UGC, NAB, or whatever), are hostile to the college goals, then the long-term future of that college is bleak indeed. Thus, holders of the main purse can be included in category (b): essential to the long-term health of the college.

Though there is obviously room for variation from college to college, the key audiences might in general divide into the four categories approximately as follows:

Crucial to day-to-day existence
Present students; present staff.

Essential to long-term health
Potential applicants; holders of the main purse; the voter/taxpayer; front benchers and senior civil servants.

Desirable and clearly efficacious
Advisers of potential applicants; potential staff; decision-makers in local government (for PCSHE colleges); research councils; potential employers of graduates; the local voter/ratepayer (for PCSHE colleges); commerce, industry and the professions; government back-benchers, opposition MPs and peers; representative bodies.

Desirable but not clearly efficacious
Alumni; ex-staff; the local voter/ratepayer (for universities); college neighbours; pressure groups relevant to education.

Also included in this category could be any of an infinity of audiences, e.g. other colleges; scientific and cultural organisations; local charities; national unions; clubs, and professional bodies. Suppliers of services might also be in this category, though some − such as landlords/landladies − could be elevated to the "clearly efficacious" category if college activities were being restrained by shortages.

This is a useful beginning, but it would be more useful still if a numerical rating could be devised for the various audiences which took account of all the crucial factors influencing the prioritisation of audiences. The desire for such a rating led to formulation of method 2. (For those wondering about the title of the method, the code-name of this text was "Keen-Greenall Book").

Prioritising audiences, method 2: the KGB-method
The goodwill test has given an important clue to the "relevance" of each key audience to the college's PR programme, but it has limited powers of discrimination, and cannot take full account of the college's specific circumstances and current PR goals. For example, in times of acute staff shortage, the rating given to potential staff would be higher than during times of labour surplus; again, when cash constraints are the major worry of the college, the rating given to holders of the purse will be higher than when the economy is booming and money is less of a

problem. A worthwhile "relevance rating" would therefore need to combine the lessons of Method 1 with a judgement about the college's overall PR needs in its current situation. This could be provided by scoring the relevance rating of the key audiences on a scale of 1 to 10, with the most important rated 10, and the least important 1. The goodwill test will give useful guidance as to the approximate position of an audience on the scale, but further thought about the college's circumstances will allow subtleties to be reflected in the "score" awarded. A selection of the audiences might be rated as follows:

Public	Method 1 Category	Relevance Rating
Ex-students and staff	d	3
Holders of the main purse	b	7
Potential staff	c	4
Present staff and students	a	10
National voters	b	7

This relevance rating, though it is reasonably useful, would nevertheless be inadequate on its own as an overall measure of the amount of time and attention that a PRP should give to each audience. Other factors have to be borne in mind, the first of which is *relative accessibility*. To give an example: alumni and ex-staff may score few relevance points, yet they are amongst the easiest audiences to reach. Each is known by name, and their addresses may be maintained already for various reasons; direct mailing, therefore, will reach a high proportion, at tolerable cost. Compare this with the accessibility of national voters, who are so numerous that a significant proportion can be reached only by spending sums of money far beyond the budgets of most colleges.

We can introduce, therefore, an *accessibility rating* to take account of the ease with which we can reach our various audiences. Once again, scores can be allocated on a scale of 1 to 10, with 10 being awarded to publics which are highly accessible, and 1 being awarded to those which are most difficult to contact. Thus we might award the national voter a score of 1, compared to 8 for alumni. The developing model might therefore look like this:

Public	Relevance	Accessibility
Ex-students and staff	3	8
Holders of the main purse	7	6
Potential staff	4	3
Present staff and students	10	10
National voters	7	1

This is still not the end of the story, though: one more highly relevant factor is the *relative impact* that a communications programme can be expected to have on an audience. Consider, for instance, the impact of a message about the general state of the college on the national voter, and then compare it with the impact the message will have on alumni. Since the voter has no particular association with the college – it is just one amongst many, and most people have little interest in colleges anyway – the message is unlikely to sink in very deeply, even if it is noticed in the first place. There are just too many competing messages, many of which are far more relevant to the individual's circumstances. Alumni, on the other hand, have a natural interest in their old college – most will have spent memorable, enjoyable, years there, at a crucial stage in their lives. Messages beamed at them from their old college, therefore, are likely to be received with attention, and to be remembered.

For a third time, therefore, we can introduce a scale of 1 to 10, to quantify the *Impact Rating*. The model thus continues to build as follows:

Public	Relevance	Accessibility	Impact
Ex-students and staff	3	8	8
Holders of the main purse	7	6	5
Potential staff	4	3	4
Present staff and students	10	10	9
National voters	7	1	1

All these separate ratings can now be put together to produce a single *overall audience rating* (OAR) which can give a clear guidance as to the amount of time and effort that should be spent on each. Though there are several ways in which the ratings could be combined, the one which reflects the relative importance of the three different scales most successfully involves multiplying the relevance rating (RR) by half the sum of the accessibility (AR) and impact (IR) ratings.[18] The result then gives a neat score out of 100. In brief:

$$OAR = RR \times \frac{(AR + IR)}{2}$$

The table on the following page indicates how the overall audience rating might be calculated for a particular college, providing a relative ranking for each audience. The intention is not, it should be said right away, to provide a means of deciding which audiences are below a cut-off point and should thus be abandoned. Communication with a low-rating group is often achieved as a piggy-back to other activities: relevant pressure groups, for example, might be sent copies of internal briefing sheets or research reports, while the taxpayer/voter can be reached *en passant* as part of numerous programmes. Once the PR manager has learnt to appreciate just how many audiences there are, and how PR time must be spread to best effect amongst them, it is likely that programmes will be so devised that four stones always succeed in killing a good dozen birds.

Those who have followed the reasoning of the KGB-method closely are to be congratulated! Others might be wondering if it is not all rather artificial, far removed from the hurly burly of chasing up deadlines, issuing press statements, and organising exhibitions. We suggest that it is not; the method does not simply allow a far more objective means of deciding between the competing claims of the different audiences on the PRP's time, but generates important insights. A chart such as the above, redrawn for each college, is likely to open the eyes of PRPs and the college directorate in a number of ways. Some might be greatly surprised to see in this example the internal audience given such a high rating; if so, they might well have been missing a vital part of any college PR programme. Others might find that an audience on which they have lavished a great deal of time deserves – once the overall pattern of needs is established – far less relative effort. Close attention to such a chart should in all cases allow the PRP to move further away from the era of seat-of-the pants decision-making, to a time when management by objectives, and sound understanding of priorities, become the hallmarks of public relations practice.

Audience	RR	AR	IR	OAR	Ranking
Primary decision-makers (front bench etc)	7	4	4	28	5
Secondary decision-makers (back bench etc)	4	5	4	18	9
Holders of main purse	7	6	5	38.5	3
Local government	4	7	5	24	7=
Present staff & students	10	10	9	95	1
Potential staff	4	3	4	14	12=
Potential students	8	6	6	48	2
Advisers of potential students	5	6	6	30	4
Ex-students & staff	3	8	8	24	7=
Local voters	4	4	3	14	12=
National voters	7	1	1	7	16=
College neighbours	2	6	5	11	15
Research councils	4	3	5	16	11
Potential employers of graduates	5	4	3	17.5	10
Industry, commerce & professions	5	3	2	12.5	14
Relevant pressure groups	2	4	3	7	16=
Representative bodies	5	7	4	27.5	6

Prioritising audiences, method 3: the goal/audience matrix

Before leaving the issue of audience prioritisation, it is worth mentioning a planning technique based on the use of matrices. Method 2 – the KGB-method – allowed a means of calculating the *overall* rating of key audiences in the light of the college's broad public relations needs; there will be times, however, when the PRP is more interested in considering the relevance of audiences to some specific goals. At this point, it can be useful to draw up a matrix which lists the goals along the vertical axis and all the publics relevant to these goals along the horizontal axis. The goals might, for instance, be as follows:

(A) To enhance the research reputation of the college
(B) To attract higher-quality graduates to the postgraduate programme
(C) To improve institutional relations with the Students' Union
(D) To increase the number of local residents willing to offer student accommodation
(E) To reduce the local hostility caused by recent bad student behaviour
(F) To enhance the level of pride and commitment felt by the staff towards the college

The audiences might be:

(a) The college's academic staff
(b) The college's full-time students
(c) The research councils
(d) The college's alumni
(e) The officers and staff of the Students' Union
(f) The local region
(g) Local home-owners who could potentially become landlords/landladies
(h) Local industry, commerce and the professions
(i) Members of Parliament
(j) Science writers
(k) Other colleges

These would be put together in a matrix in the manner shown on the following page (the numbers will be explained shortly).

The next stage is to assess on the usual 1-to-10 basis the importance of each audience in helping to achieve each goal: these ratings are indicated by the non-parenthesised numbers in each cell of the table. To a greater or lesser extent − very rarely to no extent − each audience will be found to help in achieving each goal. Carrying through this exercise systematically for all goals and audiences will fix in the PRP's mind the variety and relative importance of all audiences to each goal, and will indicate where audiences feature prominently in a number of elements of the programme, and are thus worthy of special attention.

The usefulness of such matrices can be further increased, however, by assessing the importance of each goal with a 1-to-10 rating: these are the

	Staff	Students	Research councils	Alumni	SU	Region	Home owners	Industry	MPs	Science writers	Other colleges
Enhance research reputation **6**	10 **(60)**	6 **(36)**	9 **(54)**	6 **(36)**	2 **(12)**	2 **(12)**	1 **(6)**	5 **(30)**	5 **(30)**	8 **(48)**	7 **(42)**
Attract more postgraduates **7**	7 **(49)**	4 **(28)**	7 **(49)**	8 **(56)**	4 **(28)**	2 **(14)**	1 **(7)**	3 **(21)**	2 **(14)**	6 **(42)**	8 **(56)**
Improve SU relations **3**	5 **(15)**	9 **(27)**	1 **(3)**	2 **(6)**	10 **(30)**	2 **(6)**	2 **(6)**	1 **(3)**	1 **(3)**	1 **(3)**	1 **(3)**
Increase student accommodation **5**	6 **(30)**	6 **(30)**	1 **(5)**	2 **(10)**	6 **(30)**	8 **(40)**	10 **(50)**	2 **(10)**	4 **(20)**	1 **(5)**	1 **(5)**
Reduce local hostility **8**	6 **(48)**	10 **(80)**	1 **(8)**	4 **(32)**	9 **(72)**	10 **(80)**	8 **(64)**	4 **(32)**	5 **(40)**	1 **(8)**	1 **(8)**
Improve staff moral **6**	10 **(40)**	5 **(20)**	5 **(20)**	3 **(12)**	4 **(16)**	6 **(24)**	2 **(8)**	5 **(20)**	2 **(8)**	6 **(24)**	7 **(28)**

bold numbers shown in the table underneath each goal. Then, the combined "score" for each cell of the matrix, gained by multiplying the two ratings, can be inserted. These are the bold figures in parentheses. The higher this rating, the more important the combination: thus, it can readily be seen that some combinations are particularly important and need to be taken seriously, whereas others deserve a comparatively limited call on resources. The score of 80 in column three, row six, for instance, pin-points an extremely important goal/audience combination which will need to be carefully targeted, whereas the score of 3 in column four, row four, indicates a combination of such small import to the college's overall PR needs that it is likely to receive no attention whatever. The example given is of course highly simplified – in practice, a spreadsheet would usually be necessary, to allow a wider range of goals, and many more audiences and their sub-categories, to be added. The general technique, however, can be useful in a number of instances where two parameters are involved, and will be discussed again in Chapter 6. A further mathematical model – the g-Factor – is explained in Appendix 4.

Summary
There are many key target audiences for colleges – at least 17 should appear in all colleges' PR plans. It is thus valuable to devise a method to

find the relative importance of each audience to the college, and the relative fruitfulness in respect to each audience of possible PR activities, so that resources can be allocated to best effect. A formula based on *relevance*, *accessibility*, and *impact*, ratings allows such decisions to be made with confidence by each college employing the method. Another method, allowing an improved understanding of the importance of audiences to specific programmes, involves drawing up an audience/goal matrix, to calculate the comparative importance of each audience/goal combination.

Chapter 5. Public Relations in Action

The first four chapters of this book have tended to steer the reader towards a conceptual view of public relations — towards the aspect which Chapter 1 described as "public relations absolute". In this chapter attention will turn to some of the activities which comprise "public relations practical". The intention is not, however, to produce a comprehensive do-it-yourself guide: other books in the series will concentrate on the practical elements of public relations. The intention of this chapter is rather to give a brief overview of PR activities, commenting on their place in the higher education context.

Media relations
Sometimes a college will take the initiative in supplying information to external publications, to radio, and to television; sometimes journalists themselves ask for it. When relationships with the media become well developed, these two aspects of media relations become intertwined, so that a press release might lead to journalists' enquiries on related topics, which can in turn lead to feature stories on items the PRP can show to contain "good copy".

It is easy to think of "the media" as a homogeneous mass. In reality, the British media are made up of scores of thousands of individuals, working on about 10,000 magazines and newspapers or for thousands of individual programmes within television and radio companies. Even individual newspapers, or television or radio programmes, should not be seen as homogeneous. Different journalists within a newspaper are often competitors, may not share information, and may have different views on education which lead them to treat a story in quite distinct ways. Sound PRPs must be aware of this and see that it does not work to their disadvantage.

The PRP will also realise that each newspaper or programme will have a different editorial policy, different audience, and different frequency of appearance. All such differences must be recognised so that, so far as possible, information is provided in the form, and at the time, most suitable to each recipient. A newspaper which specialises in short, breezy, news items will not welcome a long academic discourse or administrative rationale, whereas a magazine that prides itself on the intellectual discernment of its readership will resent a college press release which has been written with the popular press in mind.

It is also important that there is an appreciation of the differing time pressures under which different publications work. For learned journals, there may be no problems in spending three months over meticulous checking of facts. For a daily newspaper, a response to an enquiry must be immediate, or at most provided within half an hour. Academics, who are used to publishing only after the most detailed scrutiny of the text, may find such haste unconscionable. Nevertheless, failure to comply with the journalist's requirements may result in no coverage for the college, or − which is worse − an unbalanced report which causes the college discredit.

Press relations can be vitally important in helping to achieve many of the college's PR goals. The quality of the coverage in *local* media, for example, can significantly improve or diminish the community relations programme. Good national coverage can affect the attitudes of decision-makers and the number of student applicants. Items in the trade press, such as engineering or architectural journals, can facilitate the negotiation of industrial projects or research contracts.

Good press relations need to be conducted with a long-term view of their benefits. It is not normally realistic to expect benefits to flow from a single item of press publicity. Readers' familiarity with the college gradually builds up after a succession of articles and news reports. The long-term view also needs to be taken whenever unfavourable publicity occurs. A college that adopts an "open" policy with the press and is co-operative with journalists is more likely to achieve frequent coverage than one which has a restrictive policy. But, as the Open University's first vice-chancellor, Lord Perry, said of his institution's early days:

51

Our policy of providing full facilities to all journalists has inevitably meant that, on occasion, the University's own weaknesses during a period of rapid development were open to public view and were seized upon by those wishing to be hostile. However, throughout 1970 especially, the general tone of press reports became generally favourable as knowledge and understanding improved.

Press inaccuracies are usually due to genuine misunderstanding rather than mischief. When they do happen the college may rightly feel upset but the chances are that the minute details of a report will not register with a reader. Certainly it is unwise, except in the case of gross inaccuracy, to demand public retractions. Minor inaccuracies or misinterpretations should either be accepted with a shoulder shrug or gently pointed out to the journalist: slightly more serious ones could be corrected "just for the record" in a letter to the editor. A college that acquires a record of jumping up and down about every report that is not one hundred percent accurate will eventually find itself ignored by the media.

Publications

While media relations lead to publicity over which the college has no effective control — that lies with the newspaper editors and programme producers — there are many forms of publicity which are controlled directly. They can be used to say exactly what is wanted, in the way it is wanted, restrained only by the laws of the land and the available budget.

The dominant form of college-controlled publicity is the written publication. If there is a message to transmit, it is comparatively easy to reproduce it in a leaflet, letter, booklet or prospectus. The ease of publication, though, signals a number of dangers. It is pointless, for instance, to prepare a printed message and then not ensure that it reaches the people for whom it was intended. A distribution plan may not be as much fun to produce as the publication itself, but it is at least as important. Sometimes, too, budgets are drawn up which cover authorship, artwork and printing, but forget about the cost of addressing and mailing until the boxes of leaflets have been delivered and start to get in everyone's way.

The first question to be asked in connection with any publication is "what goal will it achieve?" The second question is "who are the principal people we want to read the publication?" Question number three is "can we be sure that this publication will reach these people?" Only when these questions can be answered satisfactorily should time and money be committed to writing, designing, and printing.

Content and style should be determined by a judgement about what the recipient is prepared to read rather than about what the authors would prefer to write. The chances are that most readers will know considerably less about the college than the authors. It is always safest, therefore, to explain things from scratch rather than assume a certain level of knowledge. Jargon and abbreviations should be avoided, and unfamiliar terms explained. Care should be taken over the length of text. Whereas some audiences will need papers covering all the relevant facts, with closely reasoned arguments, many non-educationalists cope better with shorter texts and boldly stated points. Certainly the standard advice for briefing an MP or busy industrialist is to confine text to a single side of paper.

In the case of school pupils, it should be remembered that the world of higher education is unfamiliar territory; their experience is largely limited to their home and their school. Publications addressed to pupils, therefore, have to provide enlightenment about the ways in which the college differs from schools, accentuating, for example, the greater degrees of freedom in attending lectures, the reduced pressure from staff in completing assignments, and the expectations of students to be self-directed in seeking new knowledge and developing socially.

Publications addressed at academically qualified people can be couched in more demanding language, but again, unless a specialist is writing to colleagues in the same subject, there will be a need to explain in simple terms many concepts that the author usually takes for granted. For example, an earth scientist is little better placed to understand the writing of a biologist than, say, the general manager of a plastics factory.

Format and visual style also have an importance that goes beyond aesthetic considerations. Once again the purpose of the publication and the needs of the intended reader are the primary considerations. What is good design for one purpose or audience may be wholly ineffective for another purpose or audience. In most cases, it is wise to aim for the highest quality of materials and artwork that the college can afford — though it can be counter-productive to produce a publication that has a very expensive "feel" in some situations, such as when the goal is to convince audiences about shortage of funds. Colleges have been known to spend extra money on a publication in order to ensure that it does not *appear* to be expensive while doing it in a way which leaves its effectiveness unimpaired.

While some publications are once-off productions, others are produced at regular intervals: weekly bulletins, monthly newsletters, quarterly journals, and so on. Unless these are adequately resourced, especially with staff, there is a constant danger of them faltering after the first two or three issues. One of the most common messages appearing in the third or fourth edition of new magazines, when initial ideas are running low, is the baleful cry from a lonely editor "this newsletter is designed for YOU. We want to hear YOUR views. Write a letter to the editor NOW." Producing a regular publication is a time-consuming task calling for professional skills that take some time to acquire. It is not reasonable to expect someone to fit it in as an extra to a job that is already fully committed. If a full-time editor cannot be appointed then the volunteer must be relieved of some existing work. A regular publication that fails to appear on time, or appears with blank pages, has a discrediting effect on the college that issues it, and undermines the motivation of staff to contribute articles. The moral, therefore, is not to rush into print without adequate advance planning.

Exhibitions
If resource needs are often underestimated by those thinking of producing publications, this is doubly true of those contemplating participating in an exhibition. As will be discussed in Chapter 8, which covers budgeting, effective exhibitions are astonishingly expensive. There can be no doubt that three-dimensional presentations of one's message can be very effective − and this is why venues like Birmingham's National Exhibition Centre have such a huge turnover. If a college does not take the subject at least as seriously as its competitors, though, the exhibition can be a disaster, wasting a great deal of time and displaying the college's ineptitude.

Visits
Colleges have a long tradition of permitting access to their premises and staff by other academics and interested parties. Usually this is seen as a passive activity, a facility which is triggered by the visitors and viewed as primarily for the visitors' benefit. Many colleges no doubt consider them a confounded nuisance, and discourage visitors or treat them coolly when they turn up on the doorstep. In fact, visits to the campus can be an extremely effective aspect of college public relations practice. Provided that the visitor is warmly received and care is taken to provide a relevant programme, the impression made by the college can be extremely positive, and the impact of the visit will be much greater than can be achieved through third party means, such as a newspaper report or a glossy brochure.

A sound visit programme might begin, for instance, with an explanatory tape-slide presentation, film, or video about the college, so that the specialist insights that follow can be placed in an overall perspective. A tour of the relevant parts of the campus might then take place, with visits to permanent exhibitions, meetings with the most relevant staff, and carefully orchestrated question-and-answer periods. At the end of the trip, each visitor could be given a packet of information about the college, to help reinforce what has been learnt on the day. When a visit is handled in this way, the memory will remain in the visitor's mind far more vividly, and for far longer, than any newspaper report, publication, or communication through the post.

The benefits of such visits to the campus can be increased if the college does not simply respond to requests, but actively pursues a programme of visits. Invitations can be sent to individuals or groups of people whose support is deemed to be important. Many business, professional and social associations are delighted to know of places that will welcome them on a group visit, and the secretaries of such bodies will often be grateful to be approached in this way. National organisations like the British Council and the Central Office of Information, too, are glad to know of interesting places to bring their overseas visitors.

Obviously, looking after visitors is a time-consuming activity, and it might be necessary for the college to designate a member of staff as a visits officer, either full-time or part-time. Colleges contemplating such an appointment, but feeling unable to devote a full-time member of staff to the function, might consider a combined schools liaison/visits officer post: much of the burden of schools liaison lies in hosting visits by careers advisers and potential students, and thus the two tasks mesh naturally. Such an officer will quickly acquire sufficient knowledge to answer the majority of questions that are asked, but will also come to sense what additional staff should be drawn into the programme for each visitor or visiting group.

The appointment of such a member of staff, however, might still appear to some to be too low a priority to be contemplated. It could be argued that although campus visits can make a deep impression, they nevertheless reach far fewer people than either media coverage or general college publications. In contrast to this view, it should be recognised that there is an important "multiplier" effect from visits. The visitors move in society and talk about what they have done. On a conservative estimate, for every person that visits, another five people will indirectly gain knowledge of the college through conversation. This has led the Open University, since its inception, to consider its visitors' programme an important part of its public relations strategy. During each of the 18 years of its existence to the time of writing, an average of 1,000 visitors had been welcomed − i.e. 18,000 in all − over and above the normal business visits and informal visits arranged by academics and administrators. If each of these 18,000 individuals had subsequently spoken to five people about their visit, then in this period more than

100,000 people, many of them being in influential positions, would have had direct or vicarious experience of being on campus. Some two-thirds of the visitors were from overseas, and this, certainly, contributed greatly to the international reputation that the University has acquired.

It should never be forgotten, also, that public relations is a two-way matter, and that visits provide a valuable forum for feedback. They allow external opinion to be monitored, and provide knowledge about other institutions and developments in the outside world. Bearing this in mind, though, visits should not be restricted to welcoming externals to the college. Staff should be encouraged to make appropriate visits themselves. A few hours in a factory or commercial office, for instance, can often vividly illustrate the training needs of those and similar firms, and a programme of such visits by senior staff can do much to maintain the college's relevance in a changing environment.

Speakers' panels
Another face-to-face way of taking the message to others is by respond-ing readily to requests for a speaker, or even by encouraging such requests through distribution to relevant organisations of a college's experts list. However, while most academics will feel honoured to be asked to speak at a learned conference, their readiness is less marked in agreeing to talk at, for example, Round Table lunches or gatherings of the Townswomen's Guild. The college should encourage their readiness to take part, because meetings of any such groups provide valuable captive audiences. The more that is known by different strata of society about a college, the more long-term support for its work will be gener-ated. Even if that support should remain untapped for years it can be a valuable reservoir in times of trouble.

The art of speaking to a lay audience may come naturally to some college staff, but where a panel of speakers is identified to fill engagements, all members should be offered the chance of having suitable training. A one- or two-day course arranged through the public relations office, combined with a supply of information about the col-lege, and introduction to the audio-visual aids available, can do much to ensure the effectiveness of each speaker.

Films, tape-slide presentations, and audio and video tapes
The 1970s and 1980s saw colleges introducing, on a bigger scale than ever before, audio-visual media in an effort to "sell their wares", par-ticularly in trying to attract school-leavers to courses. Some reached a high standard of presentation while others are best forgotten. Some

were obviously the product of high expenditure; others were squeezed out of meagre budgets. There was not necessarily a correlation between level of expenditure and quality of product.

Over several years one of the co-authors sat on a judging panel for an annual competition for training films and videos commissioned by all kinds of private and public organisations. In the course of two days the panel had to watch some 30 or 40 presentations. Very often the high-cost productions, shot on location throughout the world and using the most sophisticated techniques, failed to put their message over clearly, whereas some of the low-cost productions had very definite objectives and used their limited resources to make sure the viewers would understand the points being made.

That observation, however, is not a recommendation for being niggardly with funding. Through the universality of television everyone now has become used to broadcast standards as being the norm; viewers will not tolerate amateurish, poorly acted, poorly produced presentations. As with exhibitions, a decision to make a film or video must be backed with determination that it will be made at least to the high technical standards to which the general public have become used. If there are serious doubts over whether such standards can be met, then the production should be cancelled: it would be better to have no video or film than one which can easily damage the reputation of the college.

As with other public relations activities it is essential from the start to be clear exactly what the project is designed to do. Is it to give a general audience a better understanding of the college's work? Is it to encourage school-leavers to apply for courses? Is it to influence decision-makers in some way? Is it to encourage co-operation from staff and students? Concentrating on a single goal is more likely to achieve success than attempting to produce an all-purpose spectacular. Being single-minded in the briefing also helps the producer, whether in-house or external, to create visual images which are appropriate to the film's purpose. Each assignment should be regarded as a new problem to tackle; simply aping the style of another college's film is not the best way forward.

Well produced, a film or video can be an important asset to a college. It can be shown on the campus to visitors, distributed easily and cheaply to locations through the country, and can even be in demand in overseas locations. British Council offices now keep stocks of such films to show to anyone thinking of coming to Britain for their higher education. Such videos can give people, far more vividly than words alone, an understanding of the college. Moving pictures can provide even more than the thousand words of the still picture — they can leave the viewer feeling as though he or she has actually visited the college.

Audio tapes lack this important visual content, but there are still circumstances in which they may be judged more effective than the printed word. They are relatively inexpensive, and remain novel enough to be received with interest if carefully targeted. Earlier remarks about quality, however, still apply. Because audio-recording is readily available the temptation to produce an audio tape by amateur means is strong − but should be resisted. It is no accident that the same voices, such as those of Michael Hordern and Barry Paine, are used so regularly by programme-makers. There is a huge difference in the amount of interest created by different qualities of voice. If a college wants to convey an impression of quality then its messages must not be undermined by a sound-track which lacks interest or a text which fails to stimulate the listener's imagination.

Advertising

Agreements by universities and polytechnics not to engage in competitive national advertising have removed much of their freedom to use advertising as a promotional tool. Some institutions currently do not follow the conventions, and others have found ways of circumventing them without actually breaking the wording of the agreements. It is not unlikely, however, that in the more entrepreneurial atmosphere of the late eighties and early nineties, when demographic patterns will lead to fewer traditional applicants, more universities and polytechnics will opt out of the agreements, and will join the colleges and institutes of higher education in using advertising as an important form of promotion.

From a college point of view, there are broadly three types of advertising to consider: staff recruitment, student recruitment, and corporate advertising.

There has never been a restriction on advertising for staff, but there is considerable evidence to show that this freedom has not always been exploited to the full value of the expenditure. The educational press and the educational pages of the national press have been full of grey-looking slabs of print, larded with standard jargon. To some extent, of course, such advertisements do their job: the main objective is to attract people who are qualified for the post, and personnel departments usually take care to ensure that the post is picked out in bold lettering at the top of the advertisement. Very little attempt is made, however, to show that the college is an interesting and lively to place to work, nor is the space − which has already been paid for − often used creatively to make any worthwhile statements about the nature of the college. There is considerable room for improvement here, as will be seen in Chapter 8, which returns to the subject of advertising in the context of maximising the returns from the "media spend".

Student recruitment advertisements are rather better in this respect, since they are prepared by individuals versed in marketing or PR rather than in personnel, and advertising agencies are willing to show how the techniques of the commercial world can be applied in the college context. Every summer, when the A-level results have been published, colleges find that for a period of a few weeks at most, it becomes possible to attract students who have been more, or less, successful in examinations than expected. In that brief period, most of the year's course advertising budget is spent, and one or two fairly memorable advertisements usually appear — though it has to be admitted that few college advertisements have yet been put forward for the annual awards of the advertising industry. If the conventions on non-competitive national advertising are relaxed in future years, however — and indeed neither the CVCP nor CDP have the teeth to ensure that their members conform when times become more competitive — then the skills of the communications profession are likely to be exercised more and more often in the service of student recruitment. Then, colleges will have to conduct a careful balancing act between advertisements which have impact, and advertisements which can tend to undermine the most important college commodity of all: academic credibility.

The Open University, because of its special mission to attract non-traditional students, has never been bound by the self-denying conventions, and in every year since 1971 has used advertising extensively to promote its courses. By trial and error and by carefully monitoring the results of the advertising programme, it has gradually honed its techniques. Monitoring of results has been crucial. The OU has always done this by including a coupon in its advertisements, which has two effects. In the first place it makes it easier to respond: the coupon can be filled in immediately and sent off, obviating the fall-off caused by the need to find writing paper. Secondly, the coupons in each newspaper can be printed with an identifying code so that the college can count up the responses and judge which media have produced the greatest effect. Counting up gross enquiries, however, is not the end of the story; the more important figure to be discovered by a really careful study is the advertising cost for each student that ultimately enrols.

In the OU's experience the national press rather than the local or specialist press, or local television and radio, have yielded the best value. For those colleges which draw greater proportions of students from a local rather than national catchment, though, the reverse might be true. Most higher education colleges have a preponderantly national catchment, but some — for example certain colleges in Wales and inner London — have a far larger proportion of regional applicants, and of course advertising patterns must reflect this if value is to be maximised.

Other tips from the OU worth passing on are: use a few big spaces rather than many small ones; use strong graphic images; employ clear unambiguous messages rather than clever oblique ones, and include fairly long but crisply written copy in preference to short unexplanatory copy.

A third type of advertising, which is particularly interesting to the public relations practitioner, is "corporate" advertising. Whereas staff recruitment can be seen as primarily the province of the personnel office, and student recruitment is part of the "selling" or "marketing" function, corporate advertising is firmly within the sphere of the public relations practitioner. It involves buying space to tell readers something of the nature of the college, its achievements, and perhaps its contribution to society. The purpose is to elicit understanding and support rather than recruitment of students or staff. This distinction can be readily seen in the advertising of oil companies. Some advertisements urge the consumer to buy a particular brand of petrol: these are analogous to the college's student recruitment ads. Others inform the public about the companies' expenditure on research, their environmental sensitivity, or their community relations activities. This is corporate advertising. British Nuclear Fuels' television advertisements in 1987 were exclusively concerned with corporate advertising: the company had no need to sell the average consumer new or used fuel rods but it had a major need to convince them that nuclear power is benign rather than a menace.

Given the limited amount of money available to colleges – the Sellafield campaign cost many millions – it is a bold move for a college to undertake such advertising. Salford University did, nevertheless, employ it successfully in 1981 to gather support for a campaign against heavy cuts, and Aston University has shown how advertisements which are ostensibly for staffing can have a secondary corporate-advertising function. One of the difficulties with corporate advertising, though, is that results have to be measured over the long term, and relative success or failure cannot be calculated and costed in the straightforward way of course advertising. Nevertheless, if carefully planned in conjunction with other forms of PR practice, there should, over time, be a perceptible shift in understanding and goodwill towards the college, allowing it to function more effectively in all areas of work.

Opposite: the Open University ran its first corporate advertising in 1987. The media list included **The Sunday Times, The Independent, The Times,** *and* **The Daily Telegraph.**

Public relations advice

The techniques described in this chapter are some — but by no means all — of those that a PRP can deploy, and will be involved in many public relations programmes. They are tangible, can be seen to be taking place, and can be appreciated by colleagues. They are, however, not necessarily the most important contributions that PRPs can make. Trained and experienced public relations personnel can do all of these things, but more significantly can advise in areas where they may not have authority. An understanding of the audiences can lead to important advice on matters apparently outside the public relations ken, such as course validation or architectural planning. This understanding of the reactions and needs of audiences can also lead to vital input on personnel issues such as the appointment and training policy for telephonists, porters and car-park attendants. Again, the buildings and maintenance team can be advised on the public relations significance of good sign-posting, a welcoming foyer, aids for the disabled, and good facilities for visitors. Since almost everything that a college does has a PR effect, the PRP should try to keep a watchful eye on all policies and all activities. Through a quiet word here, a contribution to a committee meeting there, and a helpful memo somewhere else, the PR outlook can be incorporated widely into the decision-making procedure.

A PRP's ability to help formulate college policy is very often under-appreciated. It is assumed that academic subject specialists have both the specialist knowledge, and the breadth of opinion, which enables them to determine general policy. The PRP's specialism, on the other hand, is not always recognised as relevant to policy, nor is it always appreciated that the wide experience and range of interests needed to perform the PR job can provide valuable insights on matters of policy. A college that restricts its PRP to a laid-down set of concrete activities, treating much of the college's work as outside the scope of public relations, will not receive the best value from the post.

Summary

The main areas of activity in day-to-day public relations practice are: media relations, publications, exhibitions, visits, speakers' panels, audio and visual presentations, advertising, and the provision of PR advice. Though this chapter has offered some brief review of each of these areas, it has not been with the intention of providing a do-it-yourself guide, but rather with the object of commenting on their place in the higher education context.

Chapter 6. Formulating the Programme.

The PR audit

A thorough re-examination of a college's PR programme should start off with what is known as a "PR audit". This audit, which might be carried out by internal staff, an external consultant, or the two in close

collaboration, involves a top-to-bottom review of the college from a PR viewpoint. It will of course review all the college's current PR activities, resources, audiences, broad goals, and specific objectives, and try to assess how the target audiences perceive the college, but it will also take account of the college's "mission", and evaluate whether that mission is being fully carried out.

If there is a difference between the college's stated mission and what it is actually doing, then senior management must be alerted: either the mission statement is out of date and needs revising, or else the college's operations need to be brought into line.

If there is a difference between what the college is actually doing and what the public perceives it as doing, then there is a communications problem to be tackled.

If public perceptions indicate that the college is in some way acting against the general interest, then management must set its own house in order.

The main point to be borne is mind is that a PRP must not be expected simply to take the college as it is and give recommendations on how it can be shown to the world in the most favourable light. As has been stressed before, public relations is as much concerned with substance as with presentation: only when the college has become worth presenting can the PRP, in all conscience, represent it to the public.

The PR audit itself will typically have five stages.

Stage 1 is an examination of what PR activities are being carried out by the college, by whom they are being done, and how the overall PR function is being managed. All elements of current activities will be listed, and the total staff time involved will be calculated.

Stage 2 involves obtaining comparisons with the activities, staffing resources, and management structure, of colleges and other organisations of a similar size and profile.

Stage 3 involves research into the college's PR needs. Surveys of key audiences will be carried out − usually through telephone and postal surveys. These may not be statistically valid but will nevertheless provide some important insights into perceptions of the college, and offer clues about the sort of PR programme which would be most useful. Data will then be garnered from internal personnel on pertinent subjects such as advertising expenditure, enquiry and application levels, staff turnover, and drop-out rates.

Stage 4 involves discussion with the college senior management about its perceptions of the college's PR goals. Such perceptions of what is required may be quite different from the college's PR needs as indicated by other research, but are nevertheless an important consideration, since any well-balanced programme must be based on college aspirations as well as current PR deficiencies.

Stage 5 involves preparation of a report on all aspects of the auditors' findings. Current areas of strength and weakness will be enumerated, comparisons with other colleges made, and proposals offered on staffing, organisational structure, broad goals, and quantified objectives. Fully costed activity programmes, of various levels of expenditure, will be drawn up, and priorities amongst the programmes suggested. Methods for evaluating the success or failure of the programme should also be proposed at this stage.

Many aspects of the auditors' report have already been touched on in earlier chapters, so will not be repeated here, and later chapters will discuss personnel and budgeting. This chapter will concentrate just on the final element of the PR auditor's report: the formulation of the PR programme. It might seem that discussion of programme design is inescapably linked with decisions on personnel and budgeting levels, but in fact it is perfectly normal for an auditor to make recommendations on needs and possible programmes prior to decisions on resources. Indeed, decisions on personnel and budget levels should only be made after a good understanding is gained about what the resources can bring, as we will see in Chapter 8. The auditor must, of course, attempt to gain a rough idea of the levels of resources likely to be made available, to ensure that the report's recommendations do not lose touch with reality. However, the college management would be squandering one of the main opportunities raised by a PR audit if it made up its mind about resources before the audit was complete.

The best way forward, indeed, is for the programme designer to consider all the various things that *could* beneficially be done if resources were not constrained, in the order of priority suggested by the study into the college's PR needs. Then, a costing of each activity, in personnel, equipment and cash, would follow, and different permutations of activities considered. When management decisions were forthcoming on the overall level of resources to be made available, activities below a certain point on the scale of priorities, or which would not cohere in a cost-effective manner with other elements of an affordable programme, would be deleted.

As has been seen in Chapter 2, programme design must begin with a clear view about overall goals, and must gradually move towards identification of quantified objectives. Such goals and objectives will obviously be quite different for different colleges. Consider, for example, extracts from three imaginary auditors' reports for three different colleges, summarising their main PR problems:

College 1.

"The quintessential problem as perceived by college staff, and backed up by comparison surveys, is low application levels across the college's full range of courses. Courses which are in relatively low demand nationally are currently enrolling at this college at 40% below target, putting staffing levels at risk, and leading to serious loss of income. Mediocre application levels for other courses, even those in high national demand, have resulted in places being offered to inappropriate applicants, causing a high overall incompletion rate which has brought criticism from external examiners, financial auditors and inspectors. A number of indicators show that staff morale is affected by poor application levels, and turnover of able staff is high in spite of the current difficult employment situation.

"Since the supply of potential applicants remains relatively buoyant, overall, for colleges with this profile of work, amendments to course profile should not be necessary. Comparisons with colleges of a similar work profile in various locations, and the results of surveys of potential applicants, show rather that the level of applications is depressed by other factors, such as the college's location and adverse national publicity about the city. The college is nevertheless failing to achieve even the market share which institutions in difficult locations would normally expect to enjoy."

College 2.

"Application levels to this college are satisfactory, as would be expected considering its excellent location, and yet remain only at slightly above the national average for the type of institution. Opinions of the college amongst competitors, validators and HMI, however, indicate that the college is generally perceived as being poor in research, and lacking in innovation in teaching; Times Higher Education Supplement peer-group reviews included no favourable mentions of any of the college's departments. 64% of heads of sixth forms whose opinions on the college were sought expressed no opinion on its nature. Of the remainder, the only positive remarks on the college concerned its location and the town's social facilities; negative remarks were too heterogeneous to be classified."

College 3.

"This college is acknowledged internationally as of the first rank, in spite of its youth compared with most great European colleges. Staff and students are, by all standards applied by the auditors, of the highest quality. Antipathy towards "elitist" institutions by certain groups was nevertheless found not to be a problem for this institution, due to its association with leading figures from the labour movement and connection with innovations of recognised utility. Senior members of the college nevertheless expressed discomfort about the extent of the college's association in the popular press with the work of only one of its seven faculties. General public perceptions – though not the perceptions of the more sophisticated audiences – are found to involve excessive association with work done in the 1930s; identification of the college with such work is so pronounced that the Nobel prize-winning achievements of the early 1980s in an entirely different area are often thought to be the product of the neighbouring institution, whose profile of work, in the public's consciousness, is closer to this field."

A brief inspection of these imaginary extracts will indicate that what might count as a great PR success in one of these colleges could count not a jot in another: in fact the PR office could be rightly criticised for spending time on activities that did not help towards the college's real PR objectives. If the PRP of College 3, for example, facilitated a number of newspaper stories on the solidity of the college's research programme, it could be argued that this was little more than a self-indulgent preaching to the converted. Again, if College 2 succeeded in explaining to a number of audiences that it had seven equal faculties, it would not be any closer to achieving its real PR objectives: the audiences might simply come to think of it as having seven bad faculties.

PR programmes, thus, have to be carefully individualised. Of course some PR activities should be carried out at all colleges, whatever their needs. All must produce a prospectus, all must respond to media enquiries, all must update compendia, all must arrange hospitality of some kind for important visitors, and so forth. The entire slant of the PR programme, nevertheless, should be different at these three different colleges.

Consider the type of programme suitable to College 1. Since its overwhelming need is to increase applications to its courses, the great bulk of its PR effort must be directed to this end. The single quantified objective, agreed with the principal as constituting the test of the PRP's success or failure, might be to increase the overall application level by 10% for each of the forthcoming three years, or − alternatively − to increase market share by (say) 1% in each of the three years. Such an objective, to be reviewed by the college's directorate annually when staffing levels and funding were considered, would focus the mind of the PR office wonderfully. Activities not leading towards that objective would be avoided, even if they were pleasant to conduct, or conducive to some other PR goal espoused by a member of the Board of Governors or Senate. Only when real progress had been achieved on the application front would the PR office be in a position to look again at its objectives, and consider a more broadly based programme of work.

The programme devised to meet the primary objective might include producing the most effective prospectus of all the colleges in its sector; the most thoroughgoing advertising campaign; a college video produced to the highest standards; and an extensive and carefully targeted schools liaison programme. It could well be decided that, since the catchment was national rather than regional, a community liaison programme would be of too low a priority at present to take up any of the PR office's time; similarly, minimal effort would be put into all those duties of the PR office which could not be shown to contribute to the immediate crash programme. It might, nevertheless, be decided that an important boost to the college's recruitment could come through projection of specific messages through diverse media − for example by explaining that the troubles of the college's home city did not in fact affect the college, because it was located in a highly salubrious part of the town, and was in no way funded from local sources.

Consider now the second college, which is an interesting case of an organisation whose PR problems are almost entirely concerned with its reality, rather than its presentation. Blessed with a location which is highly desirable to staff and students alike, the college has come to suffer from inertia and complacency, lacking the spur towards excellence in any area, and failing to develop a personality. More than anything else, the college needs new drive from its senior management team. Any external presentation skills that the PRP possesses will have to be put into cold storage until the realities of the college have been sorted out. PRPs cannot present a sow's ear as a silk purse, nor should they be expected to try; nor, indeed, would their college benefit in the long run if they were to make the attempt. The PRP's first task is thus to help effect changes within the college, to bring it back on course. This is where the report of an external auditor can be particularly beneficial: often internal PRPs have been placed too low in their colleges' management hierarchy, so that their views on broad policy are not sought, or if expressed, ignored. The measured views of an external consultant usually carry more weight, and more readily alert the senior management to the importance of PR considerations in the development of policy.

Once the modifications finally get under way the PRP can accelerate the pace of change. Since a shake-up of the attitudes of staff is crucial, and a new sense of purpose is required, fine internal communications will be necessary. Achievement of a new identity will be needed, and the PRP will work closely with the principal in ensuring that the evolving college personality is well-defined, internally consistent, and well projected.

The PR programme might thus include the introduction of a fortnightly newsletter of the highest standards, and formulation of a visual identity programme (see Chapter 10). Quantified objectives could be devised which measured, for example, the extent of understanding amongst staff of the college's nature and goals, and the extent of association by careers advisers and heads of sixth forms with the key elements of the college's new personality.

Examination of the extract about College 3, in contrast to the other two, indicates that the organisation currently has no overriding PR problems. Even the excessive association of the college with a triumph of the 1930s is relatively benign, causing it no real difficulties. The PR programme would not, therefore, need to focus on any specific theme, though reference to the breadth of the college's work would be a regular leitmotif of communications programmes, and "identity management" (see Chapter 10) would become a consciously practised art. In general, though, the plan would be to ensure that all PR activities should continue to be carried out well, at the level of professionalism appropriate to an internationally renowned institution. Care would be required to ensure that complacency did not arise, and did not lead to a gradual diminution of the esteem in which the college was held.

The above examples show the type of broad thinking to be put into devising a PR programme for a college, but of course any specific programmes would be much more detailed, with many more specific activities listed. For the majority of colleges, too, there will be a number of disparate goals rather than a single overriding need: the average college might easily feel that there are, say, half a dozen goals currently needing to be taken seriously. The audit of an imaginary College 4 might, for instance, have identified the six goals previously mentioned in Chapter 4 (see page 47).

Whenever there are a number of goals, the number of possible PR programmes becomes very large, insofar as permutations of activities multiply geometrically. In this situation one of the most valuable techniques is to bring into play the matrix system first introduced in Chapter 4. Since goals and activities are the two factors involved, *goals* can be placed on the vertical axis and *activities* on the horizontal axis. For simplicity, let us assume that just six activities are currently under consideration: production of a college video; a local leafleting campaign; a fortnightly staff newsletter; a refurbishment of the main lobby as a welcoming exhibition area; a twice-yearly party for staff paid from college funds; and a weekly article about the college, written by the PRP, in the local newspaper. A matrix would then be drawn up as follows:

	(a) General video	(b) Leaflet campaign	(c) News-letter	(d) Foyer project	(e) Staff party	(f) Newspaper article
(A) Enhance research reputation						
(B) Attract more postgraduates						
(C) Improve SU relations						
(D) Increase student accommodation						
(E) Reduce local hostility						
(F) Improve staff morale						

The PR audit will already, however, have led to a ranking of the goals in order of importance, and the ranking can be made more explicit by ascribing a quantitative rating on the usual 1-to-10 scale. Goal (B), for instance, might currently be judged to be of priority level 7, whereas goal (C) might only be given a rating of 3, and goal (E) 8. These ratings can be added to the matrix underneath each goal. Next, a judgement needs to be made about the effectiveness of each activity in achieving each goal, and this rating is put into each cell of the matrix. Then, a combined rating (shown in parentheses) can be added to each cell, by multiplying the two relevant ratings. Finally, totals of the scores in parentheses are given for each rank and file. The final matrix might appear as follows:

	(a) General video	(b) Leaflet campaign	(c) News-letter	(d) Foyer project	(e) Staff party	(f) Weekly article	Total
(A) Enhance research reputation 6	1 (6)	1 (6)	3 (18)	2 (12)	0 (0)	4 (24)	66
(B) Attract more postgraduates 7	3 (21)	1 (7)	1 (7)	2 (14)	0 (0)	2 (14)	63
(C) Improve SU relations 3	0 (0)	0 (0)	2 (6)	2 (6)	0 (0)	4 (12)	24
(D) Increase student accommodation 5	1 (5)	7 (35)	3 (15)	3 (15)	0 (0)	5 (25)	95
(E) Reduce local hostility 8	2 (16)	7 (56)	2 (16)	4 (32)	−3 (−24)	5 (40)	136
(F) Improve staff morale 4	3 (12)	4 (16)	6 (24)	4 (16)	4 (16)	8 (32)	116
Total	60	120	86	95	−8	147	

The matrix gives a host of useful clues to programme design. First, of course, it indicates which specific combinations of goals/activities are most productive, through examination of the score in parentheses in each cell. It can be seen at a glance that the local leafleting campaign is judged to be the most valuable single response to a specific problem. It can also be seen that a technique which seems fairly useful in tackling the goal of improving staff morale (Fe) is also involved in what is judged to be by far the least valuable goal/activity combination in another respect (Ee), causing, in fact, damage to the college's overall public relations programme. The PRP might thus use the matrix to rank all the individual parenthesised scores in order of descending magnitude, with combination Eb at the top, Ee at the bottom, and all others somewhere between. Activities could be prioritised accordingly.

An alternative approach, however, is to concentrate on the *total* score given to each activity, shown in the bottom line beneath the matrix.[19] This provides a useful pointer to the relative worth, overall, of each activity, giving an indication, as it were, of whether or not each stone is getting to kill several birds. It becomes evident, for instance, that the free party for staff provides very little if any benefit to the overall public relations objectives of the college. It scores positively on only one of the six objectives, scores nothing at all on another four, and achieves a *negative* score on the sixth. Useful though the activity might be in one respect, it would be a non-starter in any programme which takes a wider view. The weekly article in the local newspaper, on the other hand, turns out to be a thoroughly beneficial activity overall, making significant contributions to all objectives. Since its costs are low — limited to releasing the member of staff involved for ten hours per week — it would undoubtedly be incorporated in any programme finally agreed upon.

The lobby-improvement scheme is also interesting, showing the merit in examining the "total" scores below the matrix. The lobby improvement does not score particularly highly in any one area — unlike the leafleting campaign, which manages two spectacular scores — and yet it makes a useful contribution to all objectives, as is evidenced by the bottom-line total. If the PRP had concentrated only on the separate scores in each cell, then the lobby improvement, which manages to get into the individual top ten only once, could easily have been left out of the programme. Overall, it proves to comes third on the combined tally, and this, combined with its low cost, shows it to be particularly good value.

Examination of the total score of the college video also aids judgement on whether it should be included in the college's programme. Those whose interest lies chiefly in the attraction of graduate students would of course have no doubt that it should be included, but the PRP, who must take a broader view of the college's PR needs, should not be so easily swayed. Overall, its score is mediocre, indicating that it makes a comparatively limited contribution to the college's broad range of objectives, and yet its cost is high compared to other elements of the proposed programme. This would lead the PRP to conclude that it was a marginal activity, to be retained in the programme only if resources were sufficient to support both this, and all higher-priority activities.

The *total* scores shown on the right-hand side of the matrix are also well worth inspecting, since they give a good indication of whether the combined programme being proposed will tackle each goal with the desired energy. A glance makes it clear that the programme suggested would do fairly well in respect of goal E, but would make very little contribution to goal C, which has only a slightly lower level of priority. The college principal could well argue, on the evidence of the matrix, that the PRP was not taking relations with the students' union seriously enough. A revised programme would thus be required – the free party for all staff should certainly be deleted, for instance, but might be replaced with a series of social gatherings between selected staff, the students' union, and community leaders. This amendment to the proposed programme would raise the scores in the matrix in all directions, and would thus clearly represent an improvement.

The example given of the use of the matrix is, of course, simplified. Real goal/activity matrices for colleges would inevitably be more complex, and might best be produced on a spreadsheet. This might cause readers to wonder – particularly if they have no experience of spreadsheets – whether the effort involved in drawing up a matrix will exceed its utility. The authors do not believe that this is true. The very effort put into drawing up a matrix, and making judgements about values, can be deeply educational. Each value needs to be thought through carefully, and the process of deleting, amending, or replacing activities on the matrix, with the aim of maximising combined scores, can be one of the most productive PR planning exercises, showing which permutation of activities will provide the most benefit overall. PRPs who adopt this technique will again show that they have transcended the level of muddling through on a day-to-day basis, that they no longer simply respond to whatever goad has touched them most recently; that they have become, rather, genuine PR managers.

Summary
Programme design should begin from a basis of a firm understanding of the college's current PR resources and needs, and such an understanding can best be gained as part of a PR audit. Different colleges prove to have very different needs: a programme perfectly attuned to one could be wholly inappropriate to another. A useful technique to employ in devising a specific programme is to draw up a goals/activities matrix, allowing quantification of the priority of individual goal/activity combinations. Such a matrix can also be a valuable aid in deciding which overall programme of activities would be the most productive.

Chapter 7. Programme Development and Time Management

However fine the initial programme proposed by the public relations auditor, it must not be treated as graven in stone for all time – or even for so much as a year. There are obvious reasons for this: internal and external conditions are constantly changing, and can subtly, or powerfully, alter the college's PR needs. Less obvious, though, is the fact that a well-thought-out PR programme, properly implemented, will create dynamics of its own.

There is a kind of PR equivalent of Maslow's hierarchy of needs. A PR programme might have to concentrate on certain basics at first, such as ensuring an adequate flow of applicants; this is analogous to Maslow's basic need for food and shelter, which must be satisfied before all else. Having mastered the first-level needs, though, it is desirable to move up the hierarchy. In the case of Maslow's subjects this would mean moving beyond concentration on food and shelter towards higher goals, such as enabling the next generation to be born and survive. Having ensured that needs on the secondary level of the hierarchy are under control, still higher levels of needs can be satisfied. In Maslow's scheme, it would be a matter of satisfying needs such as the cognitive and aesthetic.

To give examples of a PR analogue of this, College 1 referred to in Chapter 6 might, as a result of sound work, soon be well ahead of its initial three-year target of increasing applications by 10% per year. As success in achieving this target became more certain, the college could ease its effort on that objective and switch to other needs which now seemed more pressing. These might be, for example, ensuring sound internal communications and reasonable community relations. After more time, when this programme was beginning to achieve its quantified objectives, attention would move to other PR aspects, such as identity management, or alumni relations. The good work done to ensure satisfaction of the lower levels of needs would not, of course, be discontinued, but maintained at the levels already reached, so that more of the PRP's attention could focus on higher goals.

This Maslow-type analysis should not, of course, be overstated: in most cases, PRPs' work does not involve focusing just on one problem until it is solved. In practice, PRPs, like all managers, are juggling with a collection of problems simultaneously, some of them large, some of them small. Nevertheless, it is vital to manage PR time effectively – as has been constantly stressed in this book – and the Maslow analogy, coupled with planning systems, can be of considerable value in seeing that energies are focused to best effect.

Sound PR auditors, recognising the dynamics of PR programmes, might well propose from the outset a series of goals, giving groups of quantified objectives and programmes covering a period of some years. The primary objective of one college for years 1-3 might, for example, be to raise the A-level scores of new students to three points above the average for the sector; the primary objective for years 4-6, on the other hand, might be to circulate with high-quality magazines, biannually, at least 70% of all alumni. For most colleges, a mix of short- and long-term goals will be involved. Certain goals will in all instances have to be long term. The broad goal of achieving for the college a sound reputation amongst scientists, for instance, is an ongoing campaign, not one susceptible of short-term solution.

A PR calendar

Though a sound auditor's report should give very good guidance about immediate programmes, it will of course be up to the PRP to ensure that the annual flow of work is organised in the most efficient manner. While some PR activity is opportunistic, taking chances when they arise, and some activities (such as reviewing visual identity) occur at widely spaced intervals, much PR work can be built around a series of annual timetables. There should, of course, be specific timetables for production of the internal newsletter, the prospectuses, the annual reports, and other such publications, which give detailed copy dates, deadlines for paste-up, dates for delivery, and so forth. Without such timetables target dates are invariably missed. It can also be very useful, however, to work out calendars for predictable elements of the PR year, both as an aid to organisation, and to ensure that opportunities raised by different features of the academic year are exploited to the maximum.

To give an example of how an annual flow-of-work programme can be beneficial, consider the activities that surround the awards ceremony. The date of the ceremony will be known far in advance, and yet many new, or disorganised, PRPs might turn their mind to the topic only in the days or weeks preceding the event — particularly if the organisation of the ceremony itself is masterminded by the examinations office or secretariat. There are, however, considerable PR opportunities offered by this event, most of which require forward planning. The guest speakers, for instance, can generate media coverage if they are chosen carefully. Thus the PRP should be thinking, very early, about who should be invited, and making recommendations at the opportune time — which might be anything from six months to two years before the event. Similarly, the PRP needs to ensure that full information is received, early, about individuals to be awarded honorary degrees: media releases, and accompanying photographs, will need to be prepared well in advance if they are to do the subject full justice. Careful forward planning is also necessary in respect of outstanding students likely to achieve prizes of various kinds. Decisions might not be taken until very late about who will win a "student of the year" award, and it might not be known exactly who will gain the first-class degrees until the students have left the college. Quiet research should, therefore, be done to identify the most likely individuals, so that students can be interviewed to find usable newspaper angles, and photographed, while they are still available. The awards ceremony might well be used for PR purposes other than publicity, too, provided advance thought is given. Choice of speaker, honorary graduand, and invited guests, might all for instance play a part in the college's parliamentary, alumni, community and staff relations programmes.

Another benefit provided by a well-ordered calendar derives from the fact that some PR activities are more successful if arranged at one time of the year rather than another. A thorough photographic tour, for instance, will normally be most effective when there are leaves on the trees, flowers in bloom, and students on campus and looking at their best; a date in the second week in May, then, might be set aside, annually, for this. Other PR activities, also, must take place at a specific time of year, or opportunities will be lost completely. VIPs have to be invited to the college's annual festival in good time before the event if they are to come; the local radio station has to know in advance of an important event what will be going on so that live coverage can be arranged; exhibitions and leafleting campaigns need to coincide with —

not follow — the meetings of the groups they are intended to influence.

The remainder of this chapter elaborates on the type of calendar which might be prepared for an imaginary college. The details provided are of course indicative only, and certainly not intended as a blueprint of how college public relations practitioners *ought* to divide up their year. PR office time should also never be fully committed in advance, because it is essential to be able to respond to unexpected opportunities and problems. Nevertheless a calendar prepared in either of the two ways shown below will go a long way towards effecting the goal of sound PR strategy constantly stressed in this book: ensuring that public relations procedures are marked by clarity of purpose, not by bumbling through.

A Sample PR Calendar

(Actual events are shown *in italics*)

Jan 7	Issue invitations to suitable academics and representatives of the media to the "meet the media" reception.
Jan 20	Collate results of main annual opinion survey.
Feb 10	Conclusion of annual revamp of "subject experts" list for distribution to the media.
Feb 14	Finalise invitation list for awards ceremonies speakers.
Feb 15	Hand over to printer final page layout of college annual report.
Feb 16	Erect exhibition for "meet the media".
Feb 17	Biennial *meet the media* event.
March 1	Hand over to printers final layout of main prospectus.
March 20	Finalise plans for publicising main open day.
March 30	Submit report to finance committee on expenditure in each financial code; negotiate preliminary agreement on PR budgets for forthcoming financial year.
April 1	Delivery from printers of *annual report*.
April 2	Check for gaps in the library of photographs for publications, slide shows, and exhibitions. Arrange itinerary for external photographer.
May 1	Check students' union plans for rag week, and identify potential problems for community relations.
May 11	*Visit by external photographer.*
May 13–18	Rag week.
May 20	Delivery of *full-time prospectus*.
May 25	Ensure that details of the funds generated by rag week for charity are widely circulated.
May 27	Finalise open day exhibitions.
May 29	Main *open day*.

June 1	Delivery of annual *alumni newsletter*.
June 4	Identify students likely to receive first-class awards, or likely to have made noteworthy achievements; interview, obtain permission for publicity, and take photographs.
June 10	Alumni *"homecoming"*.
July 10	Organise visit programme for local councillors and MPs.
Aug 1	Delivery of *part-time prospectus*.
Aug 24	Invite media to awards ceremonies; include press release giving details of honorary degree recipients.
Aug 30	Update exhibition stocks.
Sept 2	Issue to media embargoed statements on student of the year and other student success stories, ensuring that home towns of individuals are thoroughly covered.
Sept 6	Finalise annual report on the PR programme, including review of the preceding year's programme, reformulation of objectives for the forthcoming period, and an agreed visits programme.
Sept 8	Send individual details of graduating students to heads of sixth forms of their schools, including class of degree and any prizes awarded.
Sept 15−20	*Awards ceremonies*.
Oct 5	*Reception for overseas students*.
Oct 7	*Reception for mature students*.
Oct 10	Conduct *motivation survey* on new students.
Nov 1	Conclude update of materials for VIP visits.
Nov 10	*Visit day for local councillors and MPs*.
Nov 15	Final check of exhibition material for technology exhibition; ensure manning arrangements are complete.
Nov 20−24	*Technology exhibition*.
Nov 29	Final meeting with organisers of music festival to check on arrangements. Ensure completeness of media-awareness programme.
Dec 10	*Music Festival*.

Again for simplicity this example does not contain all that a PRP would do in a year, but it is sufficiently detailed to show the kind of planning tool which enables the PRP to be pro-active rather than reactive. An even more graphic way to illustrate the many things that need to be done is to chart them, as in the table on the following page. Not only does this show at a glance what are the main tasks to be performed at

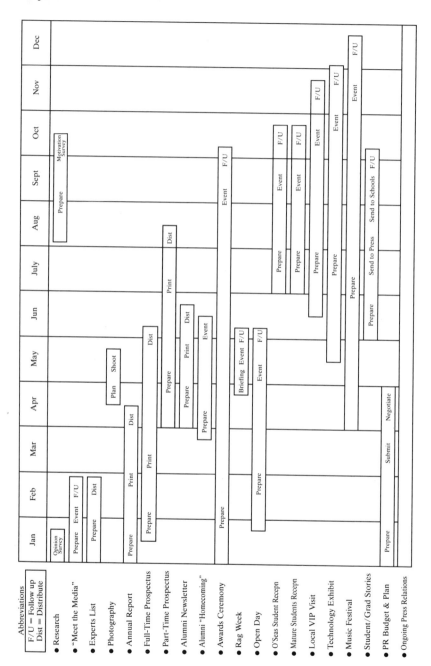

any one time, but it acts as a reminder that there is work to be done before and after an event if full value is to be obtained.

Summary
Public relations programmes need to be amended over time, as the college's needs change. Also, as quantified objectives are achieved, goals at a higher level of the college's hierarchy of needs can be tackled. The annual flow of work will need to be planned carefully to ensure that maximum use is made of opportunities. This could be organised through a detailed PR calendar, or through a chart of the year's activities.

Chapter 8. Planning the Budget

"Money is so tight that we really cannot afford expenditure on PR." How often has that been stated in college committees? All it reflects, of course, is the view of PR as a low priority area, or — if enlightenment is starting to break in — the opinion that it can be done on the cheap by a bit more unpaid overtime and some loose change for materials. Such approaches are myopic. The returns from money put into PR are usually so significant that it is highly unlikely that any British college has yet spent to the point of diminishing returns.

Cash is, of course, always found for a college activity recognised to be sufficiently worthwhile. It is thus one of the tasks of those responsible for college public relations to ensure that the benefits of a fully re-sourced operation are appreciated by the purse-holders. Adequate funding certainly won't be found otherwise, because sound PR activity, although it provides good value for money, does not come cheap. It is in fact with some hesitation that costings are mentioned later in this chapter, because they could easily scare the half-committed away. To keep things in perspective it should be remembered that the usual proportion of business turnover spent on promotional activities (though PR involves more than promotion the comparison remains instructive) is between 2 and 10%, with relatively few spending less than 5%.[20] The

80

figures contemplated for a properly resourced college PR unit, however much they may shock the timorous, are still only a small fraction of this.

Before costs are mentioned, though, a number of general points need to be covered. First, there is the fact that unlike consumer marketing, where advertising swallows the great proportion of expenditure, a major cost element of public relations is that of the personnel involved. It really must not be supposed that this work can be subsumed by existing staff with no special skills or available time. Whenever specific programmes are discussed in practice, therefore, personnel costs, measured in proportions of a full-time equivalent member of staff, should be calculated as well as the direct costs. Since staffing is covered in Chapter 9, the present chapter concerns itself only with the direct expenditure, starting with the issue of how the global figure to be earmarked for PR should be decided.

Approaches to budget allocation

There seem to be four main approaches to the task of allocating an overall PR budget. The first method, common in business, involves allocating a fixed proportion of the advertising budget to PR — say £10 on PR to every £100 on advertising. The correct "advertising/PR mix" is a frequent topic of conversation in business circles. Such a method, nevertheless, can only hope to work for organisations which depend to a large extent on advertising, such as those producing consumer goods. Most colleges have little dependence on advertising; indeed, some spend virtually nothing on it, but have significant PR needs. The method also suffers, conceptually, in suggesting that PR is simply an alternative or complementary form of promotion, rather than being a corporate life-style.

Perhaps more appropriate to colleges is the second approach common in business: this is to see what the competition, known to be successful in its public relations operations, spends, and then to match it. Such an approach can be useful in certain circumstances, for instance when a college is in the first tentative stages of PR activity, since information is relatively easy to gain, and management will be able to have a fairly clear idea about what the money can be expected to bring. Regrettably, the figures involved will usually turn out to be a great deal more than most colleges contemplate spending. The assumption of the uninitiated is that the excellent public relations activities of certain universities, and of at least one polytechnic, result from luck or a single fortunate appointment. A hard look will show, instead, that a professional unit, receiving appropriate salaries and supported by appropriate resources, is working away hard for every success notched up.

By far the most usual method of budgeting in colleges, therefore, tends to be based on a third technique: the college first deciding what it feels it can afford to spend on PR, and then earmarking such funds for "PR activity" in general, without specifying any programmes. This technique is, of course, all very unsatisfactory, and indicates that PR is still in its infancy in the world of academe. It is probable that those who agree to earmark funds in this manner perceive PR activity as nothing more than casting bread on the waters, and thus as worthy only of sums that won't be missed if the activity turns out (as they rather suspect) to be useless. With such an approach directing operations it can hardly be surprising if results do indeed turn out to be less than desired.

In reality, it is likely that most colleges will have to struggle through this crude budgeting technique before finally hitting on the fourth approach, which involves the framework of management by objectives. Where sufficiently sophisticated management and PR practitioners have co-evolved in a college, it becomes possible to work out fairly precise, quantified, objectives, and then to earmark the resources necessary to meet those objectives. In practice, the public relations practitioner, in association with a small team of senior management, would first be required to propose the objectives. The PRP would then need to calculate what personnel and money would be needed to meet each of those objectives. Finally, the directorate or finance committee would decide which of the various objectives were worth the cost of the programmes necessary to achieve them, and would allocate resources accordingly.

Though very few colleges have yet reached the level of sophistication necessary to budget in this manner, it is possible for individual PRPs or enlightened managers to move gradually towards such professionalism. The management-by-objectives approach is easily applied where the benefits can be shown, in hard figures, to outweigh the costs. These situations arise most frequently in areas such as the short course and conference businesses, where good hard profit and cost figures can be calculated. But the approach can also be adopted in some comparatively unlikely areas. If excessive staff turnover, for instance, is known to cost the college (say) £40,000 more than the average in disruption and advertising costs, then an internal communications programme capable of reducing the excess by 25% could be seen to be worthwhile on financial grounds alone if it should cost less than £10,000. Again, a programme of communications with alumni costing a certain sum can easily be seen to be worthwhile if it generates a similar income, with goodwill deriving as a bonus. Yet again, if the college is constantly running at 5% below capacity, the Finance Officer will soon be able to quantify the cash benefits of a communications programme aimed at preventing under-recruitment.

Not all benefits, of course, can be calculated in terms of cash made or saved versus cash costs. High staff and student morale and a fine reputation might lead, in various ways, to healthier cash balances, but that is not the main point: the ultimate aims of colleges are not discernible in profit and loss figures. If college PR is to be put on a fully coherent footing, therefore, and the management-by-objectives approach is to be taken seriously, then management must, in the end, be able to make well-founded decisions on what should be spent on intangibles. This won't be quite the impossible task it sounds. A university, for instance, which harbours the aspiration to be considered "one of Britain's very finest" might seem to be dreaming beyond the realms of quantified judgement, and yet quantification even in this case is far from impossible. It can start, for instance, when various surveys indicate that the university is currently judged by careers advisers and peer groups to be the most respected member of the "second league" − i.e. just below the top five. The PRP might then argue that a particular programme would raise the A-level scores of successful applicants to that of the 5 top-rated universities − and that this would allow identification of the university with that league. At this stage, we would have gone beyond vague aspirations to the point where substantiated judgements could be made. The directorate would be able to face directly the question of whether their goal was worth the sum quoted. Once a cash value is being put on such intangibles, however, some ethical issues arise.

Expenditure of taxpayers' money − ethical issues

As public relations has become more of a well-founded profession, the ability to predict both the likely consequences and costs of PR programmes has grown. This leads colleges − which are largely supported by taxpayers' money − to problems of conscience not faced by businesses. Businesses can tell their shareholders that the company's very substantial PR expenditure is worthwhile simply because in the long run it generates extra profits. The college principal cannot say that − even the far more modest sums of money involved *could* lead to damaging recriminations from some quarters.

One solution to the problem of responsible use of public money is to divide college PR budgets into two areas. The first area includes all expenditure which can be shown to have a fair claim on the public purse, such as maximising efficiency and maintaining the flow of appropriately qualified applicants. In the second category of expenditure come areas of work with which the taxpayer could, with reason, argue − an obvious example is a campaign fighting specific government decisions. As long as such campaigns were funded separately, through general fundraising, special appeals, or the products of entrepreneurial activity, the taxpayer would have no legitimate grounds for complaint.

The borderline between the two areas is, of course, often unclear, but it is wise to act with caution. Money spent on a campaign with which some members of the public have little sympathy can lead to a PR disaster if a case for misuse of public funds is raised. On the other hand, PR activity shown to be funded by sources other than the taxpayer can reap extra rewards. The booklet prepared to show how a polytechnic contributes to the community, for example, will be received more favourably if it is seen to have been sponsored by local businesses. Again, a campaign to fight an adverse government decision will be given more credence if it is shown that the college's staff, students and friends have dug deep into their pockets to make the campaign possible. One example of such benefits came to the Open University when in 1984-86 it vigorously fought cuts in government funding. An appeal to staff, students and graduates raised a fighting fund of more than £30,000. Some of this was used for receptions during the annual party political conferences, and the invitation cards carried the message "this reception is financed by contributions from staff, students, graduates and other well-wishers, and not by the University's grant-in-aid."

Reliance on voluntary funds, though, can be taken too far. Because most colleges are publicly funded they are accountable to the public for what they do. Hence not only is it legitimate to use a part of the grant to let the public know how their money is being spent, but it is in fact very desirable to do so. By the 1960s many universities had acquired the reputation of being ivory towers because only a tiny segment of the population had any dealings with them, while millions of taxpayers were paying for them. The institutions largely kept themselves out of public sight, and saw no reason to explain what they were doing. Such exclusivity was not just damaging to the institutions, as we know now: it was also highly irresponsible behaviour towards the society that funded them.

Establishing budgeting codes
Having made initial decisions on the means by which the overall PR budget is to be established, the next step in a well-ordered organisation is to designate the PR office as a cost centre, with expenditure classified according to a number of budget headings, each heading being allocated an agreed expenditure limit. The "cost centre" approach usually involves negotiation, at the beginning of each financial year, on the sums to be allocated to each expenditure heading ("code"), and a discussion towards the end of the year on the pressures on each code and the needs for virement between them. Subject to careful record-keeping and reports, the individual in charge of the cost centre will be

responsible for decisions on how monies are spent. This approach requires forward planning on expenditure, ensuring that careful decisions are made on priorities; it also provides detailed management information on how money is spent, while keeping overall expenditure within agreed bounds.

PRPs who have previously worked in commercial firms are well used to management systems like these, and are often surprised to find the looser financial arrangements which exist in some colleges, where there are no clearly defined budget headings. In such colleges, the method of financial control requires the PRP to justify individually every item of expenditure before an order form can be processed. Such an ad hoc arrangement can be time-consuming, involve considerable delays, and can lead to opportunities being missed. PR practice involves deadlines which are considerably more pressing than most in the academic or administrative spheres, and the PRP has to be in a position to make decisions without obtaining prior authorisation. Financial referral also takes away the need for the PRP to weigh up priorities, as, inevitably, the temptation may be to spend whatever superiors – who are much less likely to grasp the overall patterns of PR expenditure – will allow. Ad hoc financial decisions will lead to ad hocery in all areas of the public relations programme.

Assuming, however, that the "cost centre" approach is adopted, budget heads such as the following might be agreed. The sums shown are for illustrative purposes only, but would be fairly indicative of a number of average polytechnics, with a total turnover of some £18 million a year (1987 levels).

Code 05–01: Major publications: £45,000
Code 05–02: Minor publications: £8,000
Code 05–03: Internal communications: £5,000
Code 05–04: Exhibitions: £9,000
Code 05–05: Schools liaison: £2,000
Code 05–06: Media liaison: £2,500
Code 05–07: Course advertising: £15,000
Code 05–08: Alumni relations: £6,000
Code 05–09: Hospitality: £1,200
Code 05–10: Photography: £2,000
Code 05–11: Films and slide-tape productions: as negotiated
Code 05–12: Market and attitude surveys: as negotiated
Code 05–13: Special events: as negotiated

Major publications. This heading includes the full-time prospectus, part-time prospectus, and the annual report; the great bulk of the cost going to the full-time prospectus. The print cost of such a publication is usually

85

between 40 pence and £1 per copy, and the typical university or poly-technic produces 45,000 copies per year. Total print costs of the main prospectus alone, therefore, are likely to be between £18,000 and £45,000. This may sound a lot, but in fact represents a proportion of turnover − about 0.1 to 0.25% − which by any commercial standards is an exceedingly low sum to be spending on the organisation's main promotional tool.

Minor publications. Colleges produce posters, leaflets and small book-lets for a multitude of reasons: to sell research and consultancy exper-tise; to promote the short-course business; to develop the conference trade; to attract full-cost students; to prevent under-recruitment; and so forth. Even a small college is likely to produce 30 or more such minor publications a year. Central co-ordination of their production through the PR office allows maintenance of standards, a consistent message to be transmitted, adherence to a house style, and a lower total cost than if individual departments were allowed to produce their own publications out of "hidden" budgets.

Internal communications. Though some expenditure may be required for posters, internal exhibitions, viewdata systems, electronic displays, etc, the main item of expense for colleges is likely to be the internal newslet-ter. Costs vary enormously along with the sophistication of the product. Some colleges might produce nothing more than a monthly newsletter on a mimeo machine, whereas certain North American colleges run a daily press on mini web-offset machinery. Though no British college is anywhere near the size necessary to support the latter, the importance of sound internal communications (see Chapter 3), and the staff time spent on preparation, make it unwise to skimp on production costs.

Exhibitions. The cost of commercial exhibitions is often startling to academics; a ten-foot square stand can easily cost £2,000 to rent for a four-day exhibition, with virtually everything else − chairs, tables, shelves, lighting, and so forth − being rented at roughly the cost of their original purchase. Exhibition displays used by commercial firms, furthermore, often cost very large amounts: six-figure sums are not unusual in the least. If the college is to look credible in this environ-ment, it needs to think in terms of paying some thousands, rather than scores, of pounds on its exhibition material, though such material can, of course, be re-used many times. Greater effect and lower costs *may* be achievable by sharing a display with one or more collaborators, though it can be difficult in such circumstances to produce an exhibition which is fully integrated and harmonious.

Schools liaison. Schools liaison, which will include speaking to schools, arranging visits, and taking part in "careers fairs" and other such events, can consume a great deal of staff time, but is not necessarily expensive in direct costs. Main costs are the travel expenses, which can be fairly low if the college has a policy of visiting only schools within its region. Other expenditure, such as publications and audio-visual material, can usually be met from other budgeting codes.

Media liaison. The bulk of media liaison costs, also, are concentrated on staff time, but a reasonable budget needs to be allowed for a press cuttings service (which is essential for feedback and maximum effectiveness), for the material costs of distributing press releases, and for the various publications (*PR Planner, Editors, Willings Press Guide, Benn's Media Directory, Hollis, The Blue Book of Broadcasting*, etc) necessary to maintain an efficient service.

Advertising. A half-page advertisement in the *Daily Telegraph* costs at the time of writing £13,000, a page in the *Sunday Times* £31,000, and 45 seconds on the television in prime time can easily cost £35,000. It is thus rather fortunate, financially, that the Committee of Vice-Chancellors and Principals, and the Committee of Directors of Polytechnics, have conventions banning competitive national advertising. Though observation of the conventions is imperfect, advertisements are at least kept to a modest scale. Nevertheless, a typical small (5 cm by 2 column) advertisement in the *Guardian* will cost £205 for a single insertion, and multiple insertions, using various media, are often necessary to produce significant levels of response. Where advertising is required to maintain desirable student recruitment levels, therefore, fairly large sums will have to be earmarked for the purpose. Colleges of higher education, which may depend heavily on the "impulse buys" following the release of A-level scores, often need a carefully thought-out advertising strategy, and substantial budgets.

In many colleges, local advertising is taken more seriously than national advertising, since application levels for part-time and short courses can require more stimulation than those of full-time courses, and there are no conventions restricting local advertising. Local rates, of course, are also substantially lower than national levels – the £205 *Guardian* advertisement would cost £36.50 in the *Western Morning News*, £51 in the *Coventry Evening Telegraph*, and £65 in the *Leicester Mercury*. If the advertising is to be bolstered through display posters, such as an illuminated cabinet in a busy railway station, sums of a thousand pounds upwards are likely to be involved in annual rental. Local radio advertising, with a dozen or so repetitions of a brief theme, will involve similar sums.

87

"Small" and "local" advertisements, however, are not necessarily cheap, no matter how low their initial cost. What counts is the *cost per enquiry received* or *cost per applicant enrolled*. A £60 advertisement that produces three enquiries is twice as expensive as a £6,000 advertisement that produces six hundred. That is why advertising responses need to be carefully monitored.

It should be added that student recruitment advertising is essentially a marketing activity, rather than a public relations speciality: it is mentioned in this book largely because it is common for the "marketing" of colleges to be part of the remit of the public relations office (see Appendix 2). Advertising inevitably, though, has a PR effect and can support the PR objectives of an organisation. This can be true even for the advertisements for job vacancies, which are controlled by the personnel department. Aston University, for instance, has shown through its *Times Higher Education Supplement* advertising how announcements for vacancies can be used not simply to give a good impression of the college to potential applicants, but to disseminate information about its successes to wider audiences who happen to read the "sits vac" pages. This approach, new to colleges, is fairly widespread in industry, and may require subsidisation of the personnel advertising code from the PR budget.

The co-authors do not recommend extending the practice too far, however. The primary purpose of staff recruitment ads is to recruit staff; trying to make the ads do much more could weaken this. In any case if one is trying to affect the views of a wider audience it is very risky to rely on them looking at job-vacancy advertisements which tend to be ghettoed into specific newspaper pages. Nevertheless, co-operation between the personnel office and public relations office is important. The personnel office's messages should reinforce, and must certainly not be allowed to contradict, the messages that the PRP is transmitting elsewhere.

Alumni Relations. The main item of expense will be the cost of the personnel involved in keeping track of addresses and distributing material. Direct costs attributable to the PR code are likely to be limited to production costs of the alumni newsletter, and postage.

Hospitality. There are numerous events in the college calendar where hospitality is an appropriate aid in developing relationships with groups. A special reception after the awards ceremony, for instance, can allow some very important contacts to be made, while the launch of a new enterprise or new college unit will provide an opportunity to invite, and meet directly, members of the target audiences. There are also a number of other potential events involving hospitality which can benefit the public relations programme: for example visit days for local councillors, "meet the press" evenings for academics whose work is likely to merit media attention, and press receptions for various purposes.

It is wise to keep all such events under careful control by earmarking a total annual budget for them, and planning the year's hospitality programme well in advance. Since the major item of expense is food and drink, it is essential that events are carefully designed to provide maximum benefit to the college, and are not allowed to turn into jamborees for the internal staff: critics will rightly seize on any evidence of profligacy. Whereas in some countries expenditure on alcoholic hospitality is not allowed, the British culture is not only tolerant to it in moderation, but for certain purposes expects it. Rightly or wrongly, there are some functions where the college's reputation might actually suffer if it didn't provide the option of a drink, though mineral water, orange juice or coffee might be taken in preference, and should always be available. Even media representatives — in spite of their reputation — often prefer to conduct their work without the distraction of an alcoholic haze.

Photography. Photography is a crucial element of many aspects of public relations work. Photographs will be used in abundance in prospectuses, leaflets, internal newsletters, slide presentations, exhibitions, as an accompaniment to press releases, and to add spice to articles written by third parties. Most colleges will have access to an in-house photographer, but the importance of high-quality photographs makes it wise to budget for additional sources, since not all photographers are expert at shooting all kinds of photograph. Local newspapers can be an excellent source of fine shots, and if relationships are good, copyright fees may be waived. If copyright has to be paid for, the going rate in 1987 tended to be around £55 per shot. Commercial photographers can also be extremely valuable, providing photographs of the very highest quality to order. Such photographers may cost about £400 per day, including materials used on the day, with subsequent prints costing around £7 for a colour 8″ X 10″. Total costs for a day's shooting might thus amount to £650 or so. This may sound outrageous to anyone used to asking a friend to dig out his Zenith, but the quality of photographs produced can be incomparable. A well-prepared day's shooting, with scenes identified in advance and "models" immediately to hand, can generate several dozen extremely fine photographs usable in many contexts, time after time.

Films and tape-slide shows. Though films and videos can be extremely effective, and are in demand, particularly for overseas audiences and schools liaison, the standard has to be high. The general public spends some four hours per day watching productions of national or international broadcasting quality: if comparable quality is not achieved in a college video, it is likely to be associated with amateurism, and will damage, rather than benefit, the college's public relations. Videos of acceptable standards, nevertheless, can easily cost £2,000 per minute, but go out of date within four years: they should thus be produced only after very careful thought, and formal approval of the directorate. Tape-slide presentations, on the other hand, can be produced to high pro-fessional standards at much lower cost. If the college already possesses a good stock of high-quality slides, and the PRP covers most of the work on the script, a specialist company can fashion the final product, with professional voice-over, merging, panning within a frame, and other such touches of quality, for quite modest sums − often under £2,000 in total for a 20-minute show. Such presentations can be extremely sat-isfying and effective: it is said of the best of them that audiences often don't remember that they've seen static, rather than moving, images.

Market and attitude surveys. Market and attitude surveys can be con-ducted using internal resources, and will thus require personnel input, but limited direct costs. If surveys are to be undertaken by outside groups such as Market & Opinion Research International (MORI) or Gallup, in order to tackle audiences beyond the college's capabilities, or to produce data with greater statistical validity, fees of £5,000 upwards are likely to be involved. Costs can be kept lower by sharing an "omni-bus" survey with other clients of the research agency.

Special events. Generalisations are not possible about special events, because they will vary so much from college to college, and from year to year. Some special events, such as a guest lecture series, open day, festival, or hi-tech fair, might take place annually and thus require an agreed budget under a standard PR code. Costs will, of course, range widely. Other special events, such as helping to host the British Associa-tion for the Advancement of Science, or staging a centenary celebra-tion, will also need to be costed on a one-off basis. PR planning is greatly improved, however, if a schedule of all such events is prepared for several years in advance, and details of costs carefully monitored.

Summary
The high visibility of many public relations activities, and the PRP's normal insistence on injecting them with an appropriate high quality, inevitably imbue them with an image of being costly. In fact, if carefully planned and targeted, a PR programme should produce benefits out of all proportion to the investment. The benefits, if costed, may add up to millions of pounds, but even well-endowed college PR budgets are reckoned in thousands. No PRP should be expected to produce a professional programme for the college without an adequate, ear-

marked, budget.

There are various ways to allocate such a budget but the co-authors advocate a method which responds to PR plans that have been clearly drawn up to achieve definite goals and objectives. Once allocated, the budget should be left to the PRP to manage in accordance with normal college accounting practice.

When identified in the manner illustrated by this chapter, the PR budget may seem to be high. In fact the total may actually be lower than under an arrangement where decentralised units are allowed to spend, perhaps in amateurish ways, from other non-PR budgets.

Chapter 9. The Personnel

The role of the principal

Directors and vice-chancellors have sometimes stated that *they* are their college's public relations officer. In a sense — as we saw in Chapter 1 — they are quite right. There are few activities in a college that are not woven into its public relations fabric, and only the principal has the overall executive responsibility for all such matters. The principal is inevitably both the college's chief spokesman and its chief diplomat. It is the *principal's* views on developments that are sought by journalists, the *principal's* photographs that appear in the press, and the *principal's* actions that tend to make the greatest media stir. It is the *principal's* comments to VIPs that will be most influential, and the *principal* with whom politicians and other senior figures will wish to deal.

While a charismatic principal can be an invaluable asset for any college, however, "fronting" is only one aspect of the PR role. A front must be backed by substance or it will sooner or later be perceived as being only superficial. To perform the PR function fully, the principal needs a PRP who has the expertise and courage to see and point out internally the warts of the college; advise on how those warts can be removed; prepare a long-term public relations strategy; and provide the detailed back-up that enables the college to present itself successfully. No principal should be expected to do all this in addition to the normal workload of running the college.

Chapter 1 indicated some of the day-to-day tasks of the PRP. Ought a principal *really* make the time to prepare the slide presentations, exhibitions, and pamphlets which will ensure the success of VIP visits? Ought the principal deal with all routine press enquiries, and send out regular press releases, chasing up stories that just might have a news or feature angle? And ought the principal in addition produce market surveys, edit central publications, prepare newsletters, or carry out the thousand other mundane PR tasks which are quite unconnected with lobbying or media relations? Except in the tiniest college it makes sense to delegate much of this work to a specialist individual or unit.

The PRP and the principal must, however, have a close working relationship, and this is true whether or not there is a direct reporting structure. Needless to say, the general thrust of the PR programme must have the principal's blessing, so regular contact is essential to ensure that an exchange of information and views can take place. For much of the time, too, the PRP will have to act for the college on his or her own initiative. Decisions will have to be taken in new circumstances when it would be inappropriate or time-wasting to check first with the principal. PRPs who constantly have to look over their shoulders to check with a third party before acting will be unable to respond decisively and effectively. Unless they have a good insight into their principals' ways of thinking, they will not be able to fulfil the role adequately, nor will they be taken seriously by those with whom they deal. For these reasons the co-authors recommend a direct reporting relationship between the PRP and principal, rather than to the secretary, registrar, or other administrator.

Occasionally — though not as often as might be expected — specific decisions on sensitive PR issues can only come from the top, but even here the role of the PRP is not simply to refer the problem upwards for solution. The PRP should think the problem through, devise alternative scenarios with an indication of strengths and weaknesses, and make recommendations.

Recommendations are also appropriate on a number of topics which might not immediately seem connected with public relations. The work of the PR office gives it a detailed understanding of the college audiences and of the PR realities, and this understanding needs to be made available whenever policy is under discussion. Senior polytechnic committees, for instance, frequently debate the proper role of the validating bodies, but usually consider only the effects of the bodies on the nature of the courses, and the bureaucracy and expense it all involves. It is very rarely recognised that external validation has an important PR dimension: that the validator has a major impact on the way the courses are perceived. PRPs, who possess detailed understanding of this, must ensure that the understanding is made available to the committees at the right moments.

To give another example: a senior committee might be considering mounting, or withdrawing, a course without once considering the public relations impact of the decision. Certain courses, the PRP will be aware, bring substantial public relations benefits, and it is the duty of the PRP to ensure that this awareness is made available to the committee in its deliberations.

Scores of other such examples could be given, but the main point should already have been made: public relations must not be treated by the college as just a matter of presentation, having nothing to do with policy or the general work of the college, or much of its value will be lost. To be most fully effective, focused PR awareness has to become an integral part of the college's way of life, affecting virtually everything it decides or does.

The place of the PR office in the organisation
It should be clear from the above that easy access to and regular contact with the principal is essential for the college's public relations prac-

titioner. It should also be clear that every effort must be made to maximise communications between the PRP and the various parts of the college structure. Committee papers should be received automatically and the PRP should have the freedom to attend virtually any committee, and particularly the major decision-making bodies such as Board of Governors, Council, Senate, or Academic Board. Such access naturally places on PRPs an onus of respecting confidentiality, but unless they merit such trust they should not have been appointed in the first place: respecting confidence is one of the integral responsibilities of the public relations professional.

Whereas attention to committee matters can be a chore — and spending too much time at meetings can be wasteful — it is essential for the PRP to have a good understanding of college policy, a feeling for the ethos within which it is made, and a thorough knowledge of the constituency. There are fewer more ineffectual people than public relations practitioners who do not understand their organisations.

The flow of information must of course be two-way, and a formal procedure is needed to ensure that the work of the PR office, and the intelligence it receives, feed into the committee structure, either through formation of a specific public relations committee, or through regular reports to the main decision-making body. The latter is normally to be preferred. Though it is most important that awareness of PR programmes is maximised in the college, and that feedback is obtained, most colleges are overloaded with committee work, and creation of a separate PR committee could lead the function to be treated as something discrete and shunted to the sidelines rather than kept at the heart of affairs. Regular reports to the Senate or Academic Board, covering policy, programmes, and monitoring of success or failure, can do a great deal to keep PR an integral part of college activities.

Quite as important as the formal chains of communication are the informal networks. PRPs must ideally have the personality and inclination to be on regular speaking terms with people throughout the college, to make it plain that they are welcome to get in contact at any time, and that confidences will be respected. The PRP's presence in the college must be manifested not only in the office and at committees, but also in the refectory, the bar, and at social and sporting events. The inflow of information and views received through this network, when placed alongside the flow of information from formal channels, will provide a well-rounded view of the college. Similarly, colleagues at all levels, rather than just the committee-goers, will benefit from PR guidance and gain an understanding of the college's PR policies.

There are a number of ways of structuring the PR operations of a college, and because of the different circumstances of each college, the co-authors hesitate to recommend an "ideal" structure. Nevertheless the fragmentation of PR activities that is found in some colleges can often be detrimental. In a particular college, for instance, media liaison might be carried out by the designated PRP, though a second, quite separate, department might be responsible for publications; ceremonials might then be administered by a third department, schools liaison by a fourth, and so on. Such dispersal can easily lead to boundary disputes, replication of work, uncertainties among staff and the public about who is responsible for what, and a loss of unified purpose. A much more desirable approach is to create a structure which groups together as many as possible of the cognate fields, e.g:

Advertising
Alumni affairs
Ceremonials
Fund-raising
Graphics
Industrial liaison
Internal communications
Marketing
Media liaison
Parliamentary liaison
Publications
Reprographics
Schools liaison
Visits

A unit comprising all, or most, of these functions could be brought together by a single individual with responsibility for the broad area, though various line managers might remain responsible for the day-to-day tasks. A number of colleges have made a step in this direction by appointing a "head of external relations" or "director of information services" at a senior level to oversee the broad area, and it is encouraging that a few colleges have recently adopted the most appropriate system of all, which is to appoint to the directorate a specialist in public relations, corporate affairs, and marketing. Such a move is analogous to the increasing trend in British industry and commerce to appoint a director of public relations at boardroom level.

Nominating an existing member of the college directorate to be responsible for the function along with a hundred other quite different things is far less effective than appointing someone specially for the job: the broad PR/marketing field is only mastered through long study and much experience. Even limited directorate representation is nevertheless invaluable. Members of the directorate have the clout to do some-

thing about matters which would normally be outside the PRP's remit but which affect college public relations, such as the physical state of buildings and the attitudes of members of staff dealing directly with the public. A great deal of hard work by the PRP can be undone by a rude car-parking attendant or a filthy visitors' lavatory; if a member of the directorate is *au fait* with all aspects of the college's public relations, appropriate action on such matters will be taken more decisively than if left to the PRP's unaided powers of persuasion.

Appointing PR personnel

Surveys carried out by PPRISC and SCUIO (see pages 178−9) indicate that the majority of college PRPs have entered from a general administrative background or from journalism, while a comparatively small number have been recruited from commercial and industrial PR backgrounds.

There can be no clearly defined profile for all PRP recruits. Public relations is largely a management art, relying on the personal abilities of the practitioner, and the circumstances of each college vary considerably. After a few months in post, however, the PRP should be able to demonstrate a blend of attributes that include a good understanding of higher education; sound analytical and judgmental powers; knowledge and experience of public relations practices; communications skills both at a personal level and on behalf of the college; organising skills; personal integrity; and personal acceptability.

A career administrator appointed to a PRP post will have experience of higher education, but must recognise that a great many new skills and ways of thinking will have to be learned. Such an appointment should only be made by a college where there is willingness to provide support with funds and time off for training and interaction with other public relations professionals. An experienced PRP from outside education, on the other hand, will have a different learning curve to travel and initially might make mistakes because of unfamiliarity with the education terrain. However, the principles of PR are universal, and most skills are transferable between industry, government, voluntary organisations, and colleges.

For many years journalism was thought to be the best recruiting ground for public relations, and certainly the communication skills experienced there and the respect for meeting deadlines are valuable assets. However, journalists too have much to learn once they become PRPs. As journalists they developed an unbalanced view of PR – they tended to see it only as a matter of press relations because that was the area in which their paths crossed. Without further training the ex-journalist is likely to carry this partial perception into the new job and thus deprive the college of the benefits of a full PR programme.

As with all posts, of course, enthusiasm for the type of work is essential. Oddly enough, there are still those in colleges who fail to understand the importance of good communications, and once in a while they are put in charge of public relations. One particular university was for many years loathed by its local newspapers, because the information officer saw his job as deflecting the press and other busybodies whenever they thought they could see a story. Needless to say, most of the resulting press was hostile. If the appointee had felt a real enthusiasm for the university's work, he would have been much less likely to have deflected all press enquiries; enthusiasm for the organisation's work, indeed, is the basis for much of the imagination and initiative behind successful public relations practice.

The above might be relatively obvious; something that is often misunderstood, though, is the fact that PR involves genuinely helping people – not acting as a propagandist or salesman – and thus that sensitivity to the feelings of others, rather than a thick unfeeling hide, is needed. Nevertheless, the effective PRP must possess personal strength. The nature of public relations is such that criticism is unavoidable, and unpalatable advice may have to be given. A wholly unpredictable incident might occur during a visit leaving angry VIPs to be placated; unexpected changes in the political environment might make a carefully thought-out public relations programme seem wrong-headed; the pleasing story placed in the local paper about a particular professor will be attacked by those of his colleagues who consider him over-rated; the new college logo admired by 80% will be vilified by a small verbal minority; the response to a press question might be deliberately distorted by the down-market newspapers. PRPs who fret about the possibility of personal slights will fail to act decisively, refuse to take worthwhile initiatives, and will gradually hide their own light, and that of their college, under a bushel.

Training requirements
It is ironic that colleges of higher education, polytechnics and universities seem to have so little faith in the merits of education and training that their PRPs are often left to acquire their skills and understanding by osmosis. Perhaps it is assumed that there is little to learn − a view which rather baffles the co-authors, who have between us several decades of experience as public relations practitioners, but know we learn something new nearly every day. Public relations, of course, is a relatively young profession, and the world of higher education moves slowly. Because there are as yet no first degree courses in Britain on the subject (see Appendix 7), academics still refuse to take it entirely seriously, assuming that it can be dealt with by interested amateurs.

For some years, then, untrained PRPs in colleges have largely had to learn their profession by doing it. Often, because the salary (particularly in the public sector) has been poor, and there has been little career progression within the educational world, the PRPs have moved to the private sector as soon as knowledge has been acquired.

There is a variety of ways in which PRPs can keep themselves up-to-date and forward-looking. Some of them involve expenditure but a college should see such expenditure as an investment from which substantial dividends will be paid. No fixed sum can be specified, but the co-authors suggest that a figure equal to 5−10 percent of salary is a reasonable investment for ensuring that the PRP maintains a freshness of approach and up-to-date knowledge of techniques. The costs of courses, conferences and workshops, books, magazine subscriptions, membership of professional organisations, and travel and subsistence, all need to be taken into account when calculating total training expenses.

By now there is a significant number of public relations books available, both British and American. The fact that most of them are geared to industrial and commercial readers rather than to those who work in colleges should be seen as an advantage rather than a disadvantage; this provides a wider range of vicarious experience on which the PRP can draw in solving the college's problems. As with all books there is no need to agree with the approach of the author — even the act of disagreeing is an exercise in self-development. Similarly there are trade magazines covering public relations, marketing, advertising, design, and many other related fields. At least one of these should be taken regularly.

More structured learning is available through courses, seminars and workshops. The traditional source of formal PR education has been the Certificate and Diploma of the CAM (Communications, Advertising and Marketing) Foundation, which was set up by the Institute of Public Relations, the Advertising Association, and the Institute of Practitioners in Advertising. These part-time qualifications can be achieved in anything from one to three years, depending on exemptions. At a higher level the Cranfield Institute of Technology has introduced public relations as a second-year option in its two-year part-time MBA course for graduates. This could prove deservedly popular with college PRPs, though the costs of weekend residence and instruction are high; support from employers will be needed in most cases. For those PRPs willing and able to take a year's "sabbatical", a Diploma/MSc in Public Relations is available from Stirling University. This course, which requires 8 months of full-time coursework for the Diploma, and an extra four months to write a dissertation for the MSc, is the first British degree-level course to focus wholly on public relations.

At least as important as long courses in public relations, however, are the conferences, workshops and short courses on specific areas of PR practice. Public relations, perhaps more than any other job, demands continuous training throughout life. It is not simply that there are new skills and techniques to learn, new ways of tackling problems, and new insights to be acquired. All these are undoubtedly true, but as this book demonstrates time and time again, PRPs are required to adjust to daily change in their college and in the environment in which the college operates, and to face up to new challenges. PRPs must be constantly on the alert, bringing new ideas to the job, and stimulating the college to move in new directions. This kind of freshness cannot be retained by people who are expected just to get on with a daily routine, and to mix only with fellow educationalists.

Workshops, conferences and short courses can help individual PRPs to exchange ideas, learn from the experience of their peers, and listen to the views of outside specialists. One of the greatest merits of such events is that they allow participants' batteries to be recharged: any creative activity such as PR needs a regular infusion of insights, and inspiration flows more easily when a problem has been re-examined from a fresh perspective. The information officers' groups, PPRISC and SCUIO, each offer a summer and winter conference, at which matters of communal interest to college public relations practitioners are raised. Some workshops, on areas such as production of the prospectus, have been arranged by them in the past, and now HEIST is offering a series of one-day events on specific areas of public relations practice, such as internal communications, corporate identity, disaster management, and media liaison. Another development has been the provision of three-day courses on public relations by the Further Education Staff College, in association with HEIST. The Institute of Public Relations offers a programme of workshops and conferences also, and many private organisations do likewise. The quality of instruction varies of course and some assessment of their worth should be made before fees are paid. The fact that a seminar programme does not deal with an education topic does not make it inappropriate. As noted above when discussing books, an understanding of how a commercial firm handles a particular set of problems can lead to new thoughts on how to tackle problems in the educational environment. A one-day seminar for businessmen on parliamentary lobbying is just as relevant to colleges as it is to the commercial sector. Likewise, interaction with delegates at such a seminar is probably more thought-provoking than it is with educational colleagues.

The co-authors also recommend involvement of college PRPs with practitioners from other sectors through membership of the Institute of Public Relations, which provides such access through its meetings, conferences, and publications. A network of people in all kinds of organisations will be found who are normally only too willing to give informal advice. The benefits of membership, of course, can only be fully exploited by regular attendance at IPR functions, both regionally and nationally. Again, because the college will gain from its PRP's involvement in such activities, the cost should be regarded as a training expense, payable by the college.

Use of consultants
Whenever senior college managers contact PR consultants, they discover that in the business world, public relations expertise does not come cheap. During the middle 1980s, partly because of the call for public relations expertise by the money market as a result of take-overs, share flotations and the like, PR salaries and fees rose dramatically. At the time of writing, whereas it is still possible to obtain sound advice at a cost of around £250-£300 a day, employment of a well-established London consultancy is likely to require significantly more than this. A consultancy makes up its charges from three sources – the time of executives employed on a client's account, office overheads, and profits.

At first sight the size of a consultant's bill may be off-putting but it comes into more reasonable perspective if it is contrasted with an alternative method often favoured by educational institutions − to set up a series of committee meetings. Committee meetings, if costed out in terms of salaries, are very expensive and not always effective. It is probably unrealistic, though, to consider employing a consultancy to execute the whole of a college's PR programme: much of the work should be done by in-house staff. There are nevertheless occasions when it makes good sense to employ a consultancy. An outside expert can offer three valuable assets even when the college has its own full-time PR staff: a detached external view of the college; broad experience in dealing with other clients' situations; and flexibility of service. In addition the consultancy may well have particular specialists on its staff or available through its commercial network.

When setting up a PR programme a consultancy may be best placed to conduct the PR audit (see Chapter 6) and to recommend the initial PR plan. If it is then decided to engage full-time staff the consultancy can be a good source of advice on the job specifications, and can help in the selection process. An additional ongoing contract with the consultancy will mean that there is always someone on tap to advise on new situations as they arise. The advice may be to the in-house PR staff or direct to the principal: in the latter case, however, it is important to include the in-house PR staff in the discussions. A third use for consultancies is for help in coping with a peak in workload when in-house staff are overstretched, or to undertake specific assignments, such as supervising the creation and application of a new visual identity (see Chapter 10) or developing a lobbying strategy.

Whether or not the PRP has access to a PR consultant, a certain number of specialist services, such as exhibition construction, press cuttings, advertising, and some photography and design, will need to be bought in. If the volume of work is high there might be a case for engaging in-house staff for these tasks but normally the sporadic nature of such activities in the college environment means that outside agencies will be more economical while ensuring that the standards necessary to the task will be maintained.

Summary
The principal must act as the college's chief spokesman and diplomat, but the PRP performs an important supportive and advisory role, carrying out in addition a number of specialist tasks. The PR office must be so placed within the college structure that the flow of information in both directions is maximised, and the various public relations elements can be fully co-ordinated.

PR personnel have been appointed from diverse backgrounds, but a number of characteristics of the ideal PRP can be readily enumerated, such as an understanding of, and enthusiasm for, higher education; well-developed communication skills; and good analytical powers. Various ways of keeping the PRP up-to-date through courses, workshops, and conferences, are also available, and have an important role in maintaining the creativity necessary for sound PR work. Nevertheless there is often a strong case for employing external consultants — in spite of their apparently high cost — to complement the work of the internal PR staff.

Chapter 10. Visual Identity, Corporate Identity and Corporate Personality

Visual identity, corporate identity and corporate personality are so intertwined that they are often treated as coterminous. This can lead to considerable confusion. In the present chapter, the co-authors seek to distinguish between the three concepts by applying specific meanings to each. The expression "corporate personality" will be used to refer to the basic nature and goals of the organisation, how it does business, how it sees itself, and how it wants others to see it. "Corporate identity" will refer to the way others actually **do** see it. "Visual identity" will be the expression used for the manner in which the organisation presents itself in print and other physical forms.

In crude summary, visual identity = presentation; corporate identity = image; corporate personality = reality. Though other writers may use these terms in different ways,[21] the co-authors believe that their definitions help bring some clarity into what has always been a vaguely expressed subject.

All three concepts tend to be discussed within the college only when a logotype is felt to need replacement, either because it seems tired or uninspiring, or because the college, for one reason or another, is changing its name. Much thought and anguish, certainly, will be put into any change of name, but production of the new logotype which presents that name is often seen as far less worrisome: a matter to be delegated to someone fairly junior in the registry, subject to the directorate retaining veto power over the final design. Many a search for a new college logo has thus started off with the offer of a £25 prize for the best suggestion. Only when that hasn't come up with the goods has it begun to dawn that the task is really not that simple, and that outside expertise should be sought.

In practice, the registry junior is likely to continue by asking for £150 or so to spend on design ideas; then, remembering that two or three colleges have successfully developed new logotypes recently, the names of their designers will be sought. This will lead to the apparently pleasant discovery that there are such people as visual identity consultants, working exclusively in this area; indeed, such consultancy work will be found to be a thriving business. When it is realised, though, that the consultancies might easily employ sixty specialist staff members, including psychologists, sociologists, marketing experts, architects and economists — as well, of course, as designers — fears begin to develop about the likely size of the bill. And so they should: the minimum quoted fee, for which not a lot may be offered, is likely to be £10,000 or more, with actual contracts for colleges more often being in the £30 − £50,000 range. The hard-won £150 comes to seem even more embarrassing when it is learned that thorough visual identity programmes for businesses may involve multi-million pound contracts.[22]

The college's reaction to all this, of course, might be to say that customers of such consultancies must be mad, wholly overestimating the importance of a logotype. The uncomfortable fact nevertheless emerges that those customers are successful commercial enterprises, not given to throwing away their money. This raises the possibility that it is the college that has its perspective upside down: that creation of worthwhile visual identity demands a very great deal of thought, energy, and work.

The fees charged by consultants start to seem a little less outrageous when it is realised that "visual identity" is not simply a matter of logotype design, but rather of overall visual impression. In fact, a college might well choose to leave its logotype unchanged while still reworking its visual identity substantially. This might be achieved, for example, by changing standard colours, typefaces, layout, and rules for applying the logo, altering the type and quality of materials, and ensuring rigid consistency of application. Change of visual identity, furthermore, is not just a matter of redesigning the principal's letterhead and a few other items; virtually all stationery will be involved, and when the separate items are counted up, several hundred could easily be involved, from menus through business cards to invoices. The prospectus and all other publications, too, will be greatly affected by decisions on visual identity, as will advertisements, exhibition material, internal signs, college entrance signs, buildings, vehicles, and uniforms. The visual identity will crop up when least expected: on the hard-hat worn by Prince Philip when he visits the Engineering Department's project; on the sandwich wrappers in the restaurants; on the free knick-knacks given to customers of the conference trade; on alumni mementoes. It will be interwoven into all aspects of college life. When the total bill for full implementation is worked out, therefore, lots of noughts are found to follow the sum originally envisaged. As a result, any accountant can recognise that it is false economy to base such expenditure on a design dashed off one night by a friend of a friend who once took art evening classes.

It should be borne in mind, further, that a good visual identity will have a lifetime of at least ten years. Throughout this time it can be constantly generating goodwill and understanding — though a poor visual identity can by contrast convey negative messages about the college during those years, and pass up millions of opportunities to convey something beneficial. Viewed in this way, it can be recognised that the initial expenditure should be perceived as a capital investment, rather than a small item of expenditure of a particular financial year.

Careful choice of logotype and development of a "house style" is more, however, than simply a matter of wise expenditure. The logo will become the key symbol of the college, projecting information and impressions about the "college personality" everywhere that it appears. Used repeatedly it will build up a familiarity with the college even for people who make no attempt to absorb anything more. It will be far more than a mere graphic embellishment. If it is to succeed, a great deal of thought will have to be put into what the logo will symbolise. A scarlet, high-tech logo which might suit a new technological university could be wholly inappropriate for an ivy-leaguer, just as a design indicating stolid conformity would be wholly unsuited to a flamboyant college making its mark in up-and-coming subjects. Whenever replacements for a current logo are under debate, indeed, we recognise that something fundamental is at stake: high passions will be aroused in Senate or Academic Board, and rightly so. Visual identity, at its best, is a representation of the college's true nature.

Decisions on the visual identity of a college, therefore, cannot be made in isolation from an understanding of the essential personality of the college. This should not be too surprising. Successful public relations activity must always be based on recognition, or development, of a genuine personality. If the college has no discernible personality, then it is at risk of being ignored as a non-entity or an irrelevance, or of being associated with things only tangentially connected with it — such as the student riot that took place in the mid sixties, or the pot of paint that hit a senior politician in the early seventies. If, too, the college has no discernible personality, offering no clues as to what the management feels to be important, then its aims and objectives will be uncertain, its identity will be blurred, and support for its activities will be at best patchy. The college that is something different to everyone; a complete hotchpotch, with no unifying dreams, will arouse little enthusiasm in good times and command little support when times are hard.

Some colleges, of course, have a rich history from which identity naturally flows; then, the issue for the management must simply be to decide which strands of that identity are still valid and should be encouraged, and which are now out of date and should be discouraged. Identity management can be a rewarding art for the college with a rich personality. Where a college is young, however, or lacks a rich history, identity is something to be consciously created from its stated aims. As long as the college has strong leadership, fortunately, a genuine identity will emerge. When dreams are dreamed and imaginative individuals turn their visions into reality, a "flavour" to the college soon becomes evident to all perceptive visitors. Whenever there is a genuine personality on which to work, corporate identity programmes can be highly productive, but never more so than when an incoming management is injecting its spark of new life to a previously anonymous organisation. Then, there is no danger of the college dressing up in the emperor's new clothes, nor simply trying to project a "forwards, onwards and upwards" theme based on an unchanged reality. Instead, previously haphazard, conflicting imagery can be replaced by something all of a piece both with itself and the college's developing nature. Launching that new visual identity will allow management to clarify its ideas about what the college is and where it is going, and the impact of the new visual identity can demonstrate that a new era has dawned. As long as the exercise, like all sound public relations, is connected with the reality of the organisation, and is not being used as a cosmetic to hide an ugly face, then the effect on morale — as has been shown by studies in commercial organisations — can be dramatic.

All this might begin to explain to the registry junior with his £150 why big businesses treat the issue so very seriously. It might also explain why creation of a new college visual identity should follow a number of clearly defined stages, starting off not with sketches of design ideas, but with an attempt to clarify the underlying nature of the organisation. The remainder of this chapter outlines the eight main stages in the process. The stages are presented for the purpose of analysis rather than as a necessary sequence: in practice some of the stages will happen simultaneously or may occur in a different order according to circumstances. If all aspects of the programme are carried out, though, it will be found to have merits quite apart from creation of a new visual identity. The first three stages of the process, in particular, can open the eyes of the college in a number of crucial respects, and can have a significant effect on overall college strategy.

Stage 1.

The first stage of a visual identity programme is to clarify what the college is like, how people perceive it, how it differs from others, what its strengths and weaknesses are, and what are its ambitions. It is possible that an existing PRP knows the college and the management's goals so well that this clarification can be achieved readily. Indeed these are questions which will have been raised during any PR audit (see Chapter 6). If a recent audit has not been carried out, though, such clarification can involve a great deal of work. The views of staff and students should be sought – often creating a few surprises – and a survey of the views of outsiders should be taken. Such research is likely to indicate some misperceptions which the college must strive to correct; it might also indicate strengths that the management overlook or take too much for granted and are in danger of wasting. The PRP of an Oxbridge, for instance, may be sick to death of the college heritage, because of the way in which the college can be treated as a relic of the past; on the other hand, a failure to recognise the importance of that heritage could lead to development of a new, conflicting visual identity scheme which might only confuse the public.

A most important element of the first stage of the programme involves interviews with the directorate, when an attempt is made to clarify the goals and ambitions of the college. This is often not at all easy. At this point, says Wally Olins (a visual identity guru) "almost without exception ... I have been subjected to what I now think of as the 'forward, onward, upward, and into the future' speech."[23] The directorate, of course, want to project a sense of optimism, and will desire imagery that reinforces this. Optimism on its own, however, is not enough to produce an identity; the abundance of logos with elements pointing upwards and to the right, with nothing else to distinguish them, proves the emptiness of such visual clichés. The attempt to produce something with more bite will require much thought about the college's nature and future, and perhaps some fundamental decisions to be made. The college which decides on a heavy commitment to part-time mature student entry will require a different visual identity from the college which aims squarely at the school leaver. The design ideas for a college aiming at overcoming social inequalities will be different from those for a college aiming just at academic excellence. Colleges are, fortunately, very good subjects for the generation of design ideas. Unlike big commercial enterprises, whose goals can be simply to get bigger and make larger profits, colleges can, and do, have a wide diversity of aims and dreams.

Image

Before leaving Stage 1 it is worth a brief detour into the concept of "image". Public relations professionals tend to dislike this word, because it is so often used in a confused or pejorative manner: much nonsense is talked about the PRP's job being "to polish up the organisation's image". Nevertheless, the term can be valuable if used carefully. It has been defined in a number of technical ways by writers on PR, but the simplest and perhaps the most useful version refers to the overall impression which the general public has of an organisation. "Image", in this sense, is heavily dependent on the association of ideas.

Association of ideas is a key element of public relations – and this is why sponsorship has a role in the public relations practice of the business world. Commercial companies often pay large sums in order to be associated in the public's mind with apparently unconnected activities which we nevertheless admire or enjoy, such as showjumping, motor racing, yachting, ballet, or opera. As David Hume explained in the 18th Century, "it is a general maxim in the science of human nature, that when any impression becomes present to us, it not only transports the mind to such ideas as are related to it, but likewise communicates to them a share of its force and vivacity". Hume believed that association of ideas was the key element to understanding all human nature, and even if this goes too far, it is certainly true that association of ideas is an extremely powerful influence on our thoughts and behaviour-patterns.[24] It is not just the public relations profession that is aware of this, of course. Advertisers spend even larger sums in an attempt to associate products with positive ideas, and this is why terms such as *freedom* and *natural* appear over and over again in advertisers' messages.

Ideas, however, are often associated together for the flimsiest of reasons, and can lead to an "image" which is grossly out of alignment with reality. The only ideas associated with particular colleges are sometimes "left-wing activism", "student misbehaviour", or "sexual permissiveness" – not because this is a fair reflection of the colleges' nature, but simply because there is nothing else with which those colleges have been associated. If the colleges made a major attempt to be associated with something quite different then the pernicious chain of ideas would be broken, and they would be associated with healthy and positive, rather than unhealthy and negative, images. For many of us, though, the only set of associated ideas of an organisation will derive from its logo. We may know virtually nothing about Bovis, for instance (see page 113), but can feel positively towards it because its logo evokes thoughts of the exotic, beauty, and care for the environment. Similarly, Mount Saint Vincent University's logo (see page 112) will lead, quite naturally, to thoughts of a caring, service-orientated community. The point is that the logo is the most powerful symbol of an organisation − the omnipresent banner it waves wherever it goes, and in whatever it does. If it is the right logo, it will lead the college to be associated with ideas which reflect its nature and its aspirations. If it is the wrong logo, it will lead to further confusion about the college, or even failure to communicate anything at all.

Stage 2

The second stage of the programme is to look over the current visual appearance of the college: at buildings, signs, packaging, letterheads, newsletters, stationery, advertising, etc. It can be particularly enlightening to look at the college from the point of view of a potential student, or a potential member of staff, to find out what physical material they will receive, and what visual impressions they will gain on a visit. During this investigation it should be asked, constantly, whether the visual identity that greets the newcomer is all of a piece, and whether it reflects college reality and ambitions.

The act of bringing together all items that bear the college name is usually a salutary exercise. For the first time are seen in one place the many different ways in which the college presents itself to the public. If any semblance of a house style was ever introduced in the past it will by now have disappeared. Even if all items bear the accepted college logo − and individuals and departments might have produced their own idiosyncratic versions − the diversity of application and style will be extreme. The exercise will demonstrate more persuasively than any words that "something ought to be done".

Stage 3

Stage three involves comparing the current visual identity with that of other colleges. Examples should be obtained of letterheads, stationery, and advertising schemes, and the relative advantages and disadvantages of each should be considered. It will soon become apparent, for instance, that some logotypes will allow instant identification of the college in advertisements, whereas others preserve anonymity. The main intention of looking through everyone else's approach is to find out what mistakes should be avoided, and whether there are any good ideas that can be developed for one's own college. That is not to say, of course, that there should be any thought of copying another college's style or even emulating it closely. One purpose of the whole exercise is to determine the college's *own* identity, reflecting its distinctiveness in visual terms; purloining the identity of another would be self-defeating.

Stage 4

The fourth stage of the programme involves discussion with the various individuals responsible for producing the different aspects of the college's visual identity. This must not be limited to staff of the printroom and graphics departments. Care should also be taken to hold discussions with whoever decides the lobby colour schemes, designs newsletters and prospectuses, prepares signs, approves advertising, specifies uniforms, and so forth. It should be discovered whether these people talk to one another, and whether there is a more senior member of staff with awareness of design issues capable of co-ordinating their work. From the first these individuals should be party to discussions of any new visual identity. They will be able to make helpful suggestions and point out any practical problems that might arise from new designs; at worst, if they feel left out they might resist a new design, and successful implementation will be more difficult to achieve.

Stage 5

The next step is production of a design brief − a series of clues to the designer about what is wanted. The nature and goals of the college should be sketched out in as few words as possible, and advice should be given on what the new visual identity is expected to achieve. It might be explained, for instance, whether the intention is to present a radical new view of the college, or something evolving from the existing identity. Clues should be given on such issues as whether the design is to represent the dynamic or the relaxed; the traditional or the futuristic; the academically respectable or the intellectually adventurous; a warm and friendly institution or one that is dispassionate and cerebral. Obviously, the designer must not be asked to square the circle, combining, for instance, both a sense of cheery friendliness and austere dignity. Obviously too, the brief should be an aid to ideas and a source of inspiration, not a rigid prescription which could stifle creativity.

An alternative to presenting designers with a brief is to involve them in the first four stages of the programme, to ensure that the nature of the college is grasped in more than just cognitive terms. Indeed a major visual identity consultant will insist on going through the earlier stages again personally. Surveying the college through the perspective of someone who thinks in visual terms can be highly fruitful. Interior designer David Hicks is reported as saying "Driving down the street, I criticise the way a woman's skirt hangs, the typography of a pub sign, the new local housing. I question the way a friend has lit a room, how a restaurateur has presented his food." That is the way in which the college's physical face needs to be assessed if the visual rethink is to have real impact.

Stage 6

At stage six — only after a great deal of preliminary work — comes the creation of design ideas. This will cover a number of fields connected with the visual elements of college life, but for many colleges it will focus particularly on the logo. The remainder of the chapter will thus concentrate on this aspect of the designer's work, though it must be reiterated that a total visual identity programme should cover a number of elements, of which the logo is just a part — though a key part.

Logos can be classified as "picture-logos", "typographic-logos" based on the college title or initials, or a combination of the two basic forms. There are three main types of picture-logos. The first are the purely abstract ones, lacking any representational element. They are the hardest to get right, since few such logos manage to communicate anything, and the rare ones that succeed — such as that of Mercedes Benz — tend to stay in the mind and retain intended associations only through years of repetition and huge promotional budgets. Amongst the most attractive examples from educational institutions, however, are those of Buckinghamshire College of Higher Education and King Alfred's College, which follow:

King Alfred's College

Buckinghamshire College

Abstract logos succeed more readily in communicating, however, when they incorporate an existing abstract symbol. The power of long-standing abstract symbols should never be underestimated. As Olins points out, very few of us can see a swastika neutrally! Colleges associated with groups that have their own long-standing symbol can, therefore, do well to consider its incorporation in the college's own scheme of visual identity. Bishop Grosseteste College is amongst those that make use of such associations to make denominational links apparent:

Bishop Grosseteste College

The second main type of picture-logo is part abstract, and part representational. Since associations are so readily achieved if the job is done well, such styles are fairly common for commercial organisations. Indeed, once in a while such a logo can be so simple and yet so self-explanatory that it can achieve its aims on minimal promotion. The British Rail symbol, evocative of a fast two-way track, is in that class.

Mount Saint Vincent University

Such styles of logo don't, as yet, seem to have made much headway in British colleges. The symbol of Mount Saint Vincent, a Canadian University, nevertheless seems to be successful, showing that the approach should not just be restricted to business. The symbol is perfectly appropriate to a women's university teaching education, social work, and the "caring" subjects.

The third type of picture-logo is the representational, varying from a few simple lines to elaborate drawings and even photographs. Derbyshire College of Higher Education shows how just a few lines can bring association with the Peak District, and North Staffordshire Polytechnic's kilns and countryside sum up much of its local heritage. Cranfield's owl offers us a pleasant bit of fun: the associations with wisdom are obviously meant to be lighthearted rather than pompous. The new symbol of Coventry Polytechnic, created in 1987 by Negus & Negus, even succeeds in telling a good story. The Polytechnic is sited in the centre of the city on a spot devastated by the great 1940 air-raid. The symbol of the phoenix rising from the flames is thus apposite as well as unusually attractive.

DERBYSHIRE COLLEGE
OF HIGHER EDUCATION

Cranfield School of Management

North Staffordshire Polytechnic

As yet, no British college appears to have gone in for more fully representational logos, but their use is common in business. The Bovis logo, based on a hovering hummingbird, has been a pronounced success: Bovis workers put the company signs on their cars simply because they look so nice, and yet the symbol says, quietly, that this particular construction company cares about the environment. A number of North American companies use even more representational visual identity, employing photographs of buildings, animals, or individuals: thus do the British know of Colonel Sanders.[25] One of the bolder colleges, one day, will no doubt use their founder's photograph as part of their identity programme.[26]

Coventry Polytechnic

Kentucky Fried Chicken

Bovis

113

The fourth type of picture-logo, exceedingly popular with the universities, is the coat of arms. Such symbols, of course, give an impression of aristocracy and "breeding", which is probably why 33 of the 59 universities or constituent colleges that issued prospectuses in 1987 displayed them prominently therein. Since one coat of arms is much like another to the untrained eye, however, it might be questioned whether their employment does much to serve the cause of individual identity, which is, after all, the goal of the exercise. The coat of arms might be more useful, therefore, only as a supplementary symbol. The following examples are certainly attractive, though, and will no doubt retain a place somewhere in the universities' visual identity schemes for many years.

Oxford University   **Exeter University**   **Durham University**

When the Prudential life assurance company wanted to show the world that its staid image was no longer valid as the company developed new types of financial services (it is now the Prudential Corporation plc), it looked at its logo. "Prudence", whose stylized face is now blazoned on everything from brochures to estate agents' sale boards, is not an entirely new creation. She was plucked out of the company's heraldic coat of arms and updated. Thus might a college look to its own coat of

arms and find that an element of it could be modernized; this process would achieve simultaneously a modern device and a link with the past.

This was, in fact, precisely the route taken by the College of St Paul and St Mary, which decided that its coat of arms remained suitable for ceremonies, certificates, and other formal purposes, but that something simpler and more memorable should be used in less formal contexts, such as in promotional leaflets, magazines, advertisements or car stickers. One of the elements of the coat of arms – the woodpigeon on a globe – was thus extracted, and reworked with the college initials.

The College of St Paul and St Mary

Curiously, pictorial logos other than coats of arms are very rare in universities, with only 3 of the 59 prospectuses mentioned above employing them, whereas there are 13 amongst the 30 Polytechnics, and 33 amongst the 55 colleges and institutes of higher education (CIHEs).[27] Virtually all colleges, of course, ensure that their name or initials appear in some agreed typographical convention, and many create the visual theme of their logotype simply from an ornamental rendition of their initials. 24 out of 55 CIHEs, 16 out of 30 Polytechnics, and 26 out of the 59 universities or constituent colleges reviewed, use nothing other than words or letters, with varying degrees of stylisation, for their logos. The following are an assortment of some of the more interesting examples.

Incorporating Avery Hill College

Leicester Polytechnic

The Open University

The Open University's symbol is based simply on the letters "O" and "U", but suggests a shield. Devised at the organisation's inception, it has been used on millions of course booklets and in thousands of television transmissions, and has thus become a familiar mark of the university even to those who do not realise that the university's initials are its elements. As a result, it would be a bold stroke indeed to decide to replace it with something different. Nevertheless, in 1987 the university decided to call in a firm of consultants to look at it afresh and review its application throughout the organisation. Two main problems had emerged. Initially the logo had been designed primarily with stationery in mind. The typeface chosen for the university's name was entirely suitable for this purpose, being elegant and giving an impression of respectability at a time when the university was being ridiculed because of the unorthodoxy of its proposed teaching methods and its open entry philosophy. The logo also proved to work well on the printed course materials and on the television screen. However, over the years it was found to be unsuitable for other purposes such as advertisements, exhibitions, and applications where a much bolder impact was required. Furthermore no clear guidelines had been laid down as to how the logo should be used. Consequently, the shape of the shield varied from time to time and a whole variety of typefaces came into use for the university's name. There was also the thought that as the OU had changed considerably in many ways since the early days, the time might have come for a designer to advise whether the original logo still reflected adequately the present nature of the university.

As this book went to press the exercise was still in progress, but it was likely that a complete departure from the original shield would be avoided because of the recognition and goodwill it had achieved. A more probable outcome was that a modern face-lift would be devised and rules adopted for its use in different applications. Such gradual evolution of a logo, which retains associations while allowing for development as tastes and times change, is a common phenomenon. The transition of the logo of the Automobile Association is an example. There really was no way that the original logo could have remained unchanged throughout the sixties and seventies, however attractive it might have seemed in the early years.

Though the Oxford Polytechnic logo has built up a great deal less public recognition than that of either the AA or the Open University, the objective of retaining an identity through evolution commended itself to planners during its two redesigns over the period 1982 – 1986. The first of the logos shown below had achieved its initial goal of being distinctive, but had met with practical problems. In advertisements, for instance, the lines tended to fill in, and whenever printed on a small scale, the design would seem over-fussy. This was the main reason for its redesign in a bolder and simpler form. The original design had, however, been adopted by Letraset[28] (who referred to it, predictably, as

"Oxford" – a common fate of initiatives emanating from Oxford Polytechnic) and used widely by many commercial companies. Instead of
being recognised, therefore, as distinctive, the 1983 Oxford Polytechnic
logo came to appear as nothing more than yet another derivative of the
Letraset catalogue! The solution to this was to rework the original
design once more, to recover the lost distinctiveness.

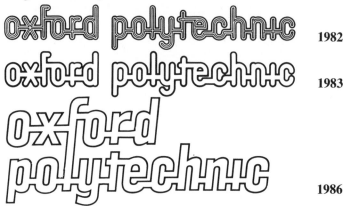

1982

1983

1986

Another merit of reworking an existing design is that it will meet with a
far less difficult reception from the internal audience than a completely
new one. Where symbols are concerned, people tend to be happier to
stick, so far as possible, with what they know. Even in cases of gentle
transition, though, the designer will do well to arrange regular meetings
with the main college contacts – particularly the PRP and the principal
– to see which of the variations are really worth developing, and which
are not viable. The PRP in particular will need to keep an eye on
whether amendments are likely to be politically acceptable, just as it is
necessary to remain alert to whether they will work technically, or will
require excessive expense to implement.

Stage 7
The penultimate stage is the presentation. At this point, the fully
worked out design, agreed by the PRP and principal, is shown to wide
audiences. The intention is to "sell" the design to everyone within the
college, so that it can be implemented with common consent. Officially,
the main presentation – to Council, Senate, or Academic Board – is
for approval: if the members are just told what they are to get, their co-
operation may not be forthcoming. The presentation, thus, needs to be
thorough, showing all the advantages of the new system, preferably with
graphic aids to highlight the weaknesses of the present system. Because

widespread approval for the new scheme is essential for a successful implementation, lobbying of key figures is sometimes carried out in advance. Presentation should not take place until a safe passage is reasonably certain. It is unwise to offer the board members genuine alternatives from which to chose – except for the choice of staying with the existing logo. Choosing between genuine new alternatives at this late stage could lead to choice of a "safe" design which neither offends nor pleases anyone, or a division of opinion which loses the unified support for the new visual identity that is essential to its success.

The presentation, since it must evoke enthusiasm, should to some extent be a bit of theatre. A series of subsidiary presentations will also need to take place, so that everyone throughout the organisation is supportive, and recognises how the changes will affect them. There is merit, therefore, in producing from the start a solid presentation show, fully backed by an audio-visual demonstration and prototype design manuals. A pull-out section of the college newsletter can provide useful additional back-up. Throughout, the fundamental reasons for the change should be given; the affair must not be trivialised. External launches, however, can be dangerous, even if the new visual identity is of the highest standard: it is very tempting, and very easy, for outsiders to mock at fuss over "a mere logo", as Birmingham Polytechnic discovered in June 1987.[29] Introduction of the new scheme will certainly produce publicity, however, and opportunities for positive exposure should be seized.

Stage 8
The final stage of the programme is implementation. If external consultants have been appointed and are still involved at this point – and they certainly should be, or the PRP will be left with a huge amount of work – a design manual will be produced to show how the new visual identity is to be manifested in all predictable circumstances. Implementation will certainly be more successful if the design team have correctly anticipated practical difficulties and provided variations of the basic design to meet those problems. A logo might, for instance, be offered in right-, left-, and centre-justified forms to meet varying needs. A complex design should also be offered in a simplified version, so that it can appear, for instance, in small newspaper advertisements where ink will smudge. If the basic logo involves several colours, then a monochrome variation should also be prepared. If the typography is original, then an alphabet will need to be added so that signs and printed headings can follow the same style.

Once agreed, the visual identity has to be implemented with the full authority of a major college decision. If the exercise has been handled seriously a great deal of thought and probably much money will have been expended to arrive at something which will stand as the public face of the college for years to come. The manual's guidelines should be regarded not as advisory but as mandatory. They will have tried to encompass all applications but it is important that someone with the full backing of the principal is designated as being responsible for handling any problems. Whoever that person is, he or she must have the authority to stamp out misuse. Individuals must not be allowed to continue using the old logo because they prefer it; nobody should get away with adding their own idiosyncratic flourishes; conflicting internal signs put up by well-meaning amateurs must be taken down immediately. Care must also be taken to ensure that manifestations of the new designs are looked after. The impressive new logos on the side of the college vehicles will do nothing for the organisation if they are rarely washed, nor will the new college sign be impressive for long if the graffiti is not removed. Without an authoritative overseer, the advantages and unification offered by the new visual identity will never be realised, nor will the reinforcement that springs from consistent repetition be fully achieved.

Often enough, of course, the PRP will be in charge of implementation, and a number of unexpected problems will have to be faced. An extraordinary number of uses for the new design will be involved, not all of which can have been foreseen, each requiring investigation and careful interpretation of the design manual. Without sufficient support, the workload can be such that implementation has to be curtailed immediately after production of the letterheads, for simple lack of time. In some colleges it will also be found that the quality of the internal printroom's work is far below the desired standard. Printrooms in most colleges spend the great bulk of their time duplicating committee and teaching materials, where turn-round time is crucial, but visual quality is not necessarily an important factor. When faced with the need to produce sophisticated products, few college printrooms cope even as well, qualitatively, as the high-street printer. This, allied with the volume of extra work, can put internal staff under pressures with which they cannot cope. The only solution, except for the rare college with excellent in-house facilities with no capacity problems, is to employ a good outside printer, and an external design team that can be trusted to interpret the visual identity scheme correctly.[30]

Note
However deep its corporate personality thinking, and however fine its visual identity programme might be, any college will continue to draw much of its corporate identity from the sector of which it is a part. A

university will have the identity, first and foremost, of a university, just as polytechnics and colleges of higher education will be seen primarily as manifestations of the wider movements. Individual colleges should thus remind themselves that although they have their own unique characteristics, there is much to be gained from identification with fellow colleges in their own sector. They need to maintain an appropriate identity programme for the sector as a whole, and recognise that support for such activities represents, not altruism, but enlightened self-interest.

Summary
The three expressions "corporate personality", "corporate identity" and "visual identity", though often used as synonymous, each have a different meaning. The visual identity of a college is often treated as something of minor importance, and yet it heavily influences the perceptions of the college amongst its various audiences. The task of revising the visual identity should not be underestimated. A successful logotype, combined with other elements of the visual identity scheme, will have to be devised with great care if the desired impressions of the college are to be conveyed.

Eight main stages are involved in a visual identity programme. The first involves a study of the college's nature, distinctive features, and ambitions. A successful identity programme must be based on projection of a genuine college personality, not on application of cosmetics to something featureless. The second and third stages involve analysing the current visual appearance of the college and comparing this with the visual identity of other colleges. Stage four involves discovering, and gaining feedback from, the various individuals controlling the different aspects of the college's visual identity.

Having gained an understanding of the nature of the problem through the above stages, a design brief can be written to guide the designer — the fifth stage in the process. Design ideas then flow, at stage six. Much work at this point will focus on the creation of logotypes, which may be based on abstract designs, on the representational, or on typographical variants of the college name. Having finalised designs found acceptable to the principal and PRP, the seventh stage in the programme is a presentation aimed at explaining to the internal audience the advantages of the new scheme, and gaining their co-operation in its implementation. Implementation is the eighth and last stage in the process. The scale of this task should not be underestimated: an astonishingly wide number of items will be involved. In order to ensure that the full advantages of the new visual identity are gained, thorough oversight of the implementation process is essential.

Chapter 11. Issue and Crisis Management

In the continuing development of public relations as a management art, professionals have been paying increasing attention to two important concepts: *issue management* and *crisis management*. Both are essentially concerned with the future rather than the present: both require a pro-active rather than reactive approach. Management by anticipation, rather than management by crisis, is now seen to be necessary even for the management of crisis itself.

Issue management
Issue management is the art of monitoring social trends, external events and shifts of opinion which might have a future impact on the organisation. For a commercial firm these might, for instance, be the influence of environmental protection groups, the militance or otherwise of trade unions, unemployment, consumerism, and political changes. The management art is on the one hand to assess whether the trends provide opportunities that can be exploited in some way to the benefit of the company; on the other hand it is to prepare the company in advance to deal with adverse happenings. A noticeable increase in public concern about food additives, for example, should prompt a food company to explore how in future it could provide more natural foods. Falling unemployment should alert labour-intensive industries to the fact that

122

they might have a recruitment problem in a few years' time and should make plans accordingly.

Because commercial PRPs are the individuals particularly concerned with their organisation's place in society, it is natural for them to play leading roles in this planning process. They thus commonly set up systems for gathering intelligence about what is happening in the outside world, analyse it, and with management colleagues, consider what action should be taken. Complacent college PRPs might feel that all this is far removed from life in their own environment. If so, they are mistaken. There are many issues and trends which affect the future of a college. Some are internal, some are local, some are national and some are international.

Will cut-backs in local bus services make student residences inaccessible? If demographic statistics indicate a shortage of school leavers in five years time, should the college now be enhancing its programme for mature students? If low academic salaries are causing discontent, will there be a shortage of specialist lecturers in two years time? Is there a change in the national culture which the college is not recognising in its syllabus, and which will leave it over-dependent on declining subject areas? Are student politics likely to impede the freedom of visiting speakers? Has the college any South African connections that might offend anti-apartheid groups? How will a change of government affect the college's profile of work and income? What European legislation — for example on credit transfer, parity of qualifications, fee levels, or travel schemes — will affect the college in the next decade?

Since the above are only a selection of the questions which could be raised, it can be seen to be naive to treat issue management as a question only for commercial PRPs. Such topics have important consequences not only for the shape of a college in the future, but also, possibly, for its very survival. The PRP must ensure, therefore, that they are being studied in the college systematically.

Crisis management
Crisis management used to be viewed as the art of dealing with a disaster once it had struck: more correctly, though, it should be perceived as the art of preparing the company in advance to deal with things that might suddenly go wrong. For large corporations, it would be singularly inept to start thinking about how a disaster should be handled after an air crash had occurred with serious loss of life, an oil tanker had run aground and was polluting beaches, a customer had died because of a faulty product, or a financial scandal had erupted involving top management. When the organisation has the world's press clamouring for information and comment there is no time to convene lengthy board

meetings, call in advisers, and prepare policies on how it should all be handled.

Large corporations therefore prepare scenarios of how they would handle specific disasters, and formulate general plans for dealing with contingencies which cannot be clearly identified in advance. Some companies, including the oil giants, even subject their management teams to exercises in which disasters are simulated. As part of these exercises actors and outside specialists, such as journalists and investment analysts, are brought in to test the companies' systems and the reactions of the individuals who would find themselves in the hot seat during the real-life situations.

Smaller organisations will not normally expect to conduct contingency planning on such a scale, and yet crisis management certainly has a place within them. In the case of colleges, the number of public relations crises experienced over the last twenty years should make such a need evident. In fact, public relations practice in British higher education was to some extent born out of the experience of such traumas: the days of student activism often led to a great deal of negative media coverage, sometimes causing considerable damage, and PR appointments were subsequently made with the aim of preventing repetition of painful episodes. PRPs hired in this manner sometimes felt that they had been appointed as a kind of official talisman to deflect the ill will of the gods from their colleges' walls. There was obviously a limit to what could be done, but with sufficient planning, damage to the college could at least be minimised, and in some cases, forward planning could allow difficult episodes to be avoided altogether.

PR disasters and crises undergone by other colleges are well worth studying for the lessons that they can provide. Many different kinds have arisen. Major fires have broken out; rag stunts have by ill-luck gone wrong; principals have died suddenly; students have had tragic accidents; wrong examination results have been allocated; rent strikes have taken place. It is at times like these that the college is suddenly thrust into the limelight. How it behaves in such circumstances will determine whether it receives public condemnation or sympathy. Internally, the confidence that stems from handling a crisis well will do much to counter the setback that has been caused. On the other hand, handling it badly, particularly in the glare of public interest, will make the situation even worse.

PR writers have classified crises as "known unknowns" and "unknown unknowns". The "known unknowns" are the events which are predictable in kind, though nobody knows when they will happen. Sooner or later, for instance, every college will be faced with misbehaviour towards a visiting VIP, but it may happen in weeks, months, or in thirty years time. Abuse of drugs by students, again, is a problem that can arise at any time, leading to damaging media coverage: in any community of thousands, there is always a tiny minority whose actions can cause damage to the reputation of the group. Other crises, too, can be calculated to be more or less probable. When animal liberation first led to militant actions, the first universities to be raided were caught unawares, and found themselves having to deal, not always successfully, with demonstrations on campus, personal threats to researchers, and hostile media stories about vivisection. Other colleges which kept their wits about them were able to read the signs, and take a number of steps to minimise the dangers.

The "unknown unknowns" are the crises whose nature is wholly unpredictable. The college registrar who turns out to be a Nazi war criminal, or the bizarre accident on campus befalling the cabinet minister's son, will lead to problems which could not be foreseen in detail. Nevertheless, forward thought can ensure that there is a general contingency plan to be followed. At the very least the college should arrange an agreed channel of communications for such crises, with home telephone numbers known to all key personnel, so that the college will act responsibly and speedily, and be seen to be so acting. Damage is reduced by ensuring that the media do not have to resort to interviewing unauthorised college staff, but rather are met with open, unpanicked, and quickly responsive official sources. If the college has previously enjoyed a good relationship with the media, then continued openness will help ensure that coverage is reasonably sympathetic. On the other hand, if the college's previous relationship with the media has been bad, nobody should be surprised if the occasion is used to heap on extra embarrassment.

While this book has been at pains to stress that media relations is only one of the PRP's concerns, in time of crisis it is plainly one of the most important, and will thus figure prominently in the college's overall preparations for crises. It is by no means the only concern, however. There are other audiences to consider in the planning of communications: for example relevant internal staff, emergency services, and members of the governing body. Where a tragedy is concerned, it is important that the relatives of those involved should not be left to hear about it from the media. Members of the college, also, have a natural right to receive authoritative details at the earliest possible time.

Forward planning

In planning for a crisis there are several distinct actions to be taken:

1. Think of as many things as possible that can go wrong: fire, building collapse, demonstrations, occupations, nuclear radiation, atmosphe-

ric pollution, animal escapes, food poisoning, laboratory accidents, crime, scandals covering members of staff, etc.

2. Establish a communications chain. Several key people need to be informed immediately a crisis occurs: the principal, secretary, and PRP for all events, while others – such as the safety officer, buildings officer, medical officer, and the chairman of governors – may need to be contacted quickly for specific events.

3. Establish a routine for identifying and communicating with all affected audiences.

4. Nominate and train appropriate spokespersons for handling media enquiries. (At least one senior officer – the principal or deputy principal – should have had specialist coaching on how to cope with TV interviews.)

5. Prepare college policy statements in advance to be used as appropriate: for example on health and safety, on back-up systems for computers, and on appointment and disciplinary procedures for senior members of staff.

6. Appoint a "crisis management group" which can be assembled quickly to make emergency decisions. This should have a core of the principal, secretary and PRP for *all* crises, with others being added ad hoc for specific crises.

7. Offer some training to key personnel in handling crises, and ideally set up simulation exercises.

8. Prepare clear instructions for security staff on what to do initially.

In thinking through specific problems that might occur, it is well worth writing up checklists of relevant points. For example, when considering the implications of potential student misbehaviour during VIP visits, the following might be prepared for discussion with senior management:

1. Can the PR office be sure that it knows when student groups and others invite VIPs onto campus?

2. Is there a method for vetting the room bookings made by outside organisations?

3. Has the college devised satisfactory communications with the police concerning VIP visits?

4. If the VIP is likely to evoke confrontation, will there be sufficient security staff on hand?

5. Is the college code of conduct clear about the standards of behaviour to be expected of students? Is the disciplinary procedure adequate, and can it be seen to be adequate?

6. Will a responsible member of staff with PR clearance be on hand throughout the more contentious visits?

7. Is a procedure in place allowing official statements to be produced by the college, 24 hours a day, 365 days a year?

In the case of animal welfare, the following checklist might be written up:

1. Are all legal requirements concerning animal welfare followed scrupulously?

2. Does a written justification of all work involving the use of animals exist? Is there a system for reviewing the necessity of all animal work? Does the college's research profile make an ethics committee necessary?

3. Is the training and supervision of all members of staff involved in animal work beyond reproach?

4. Is there a clear statement to potential students of biology and related subjects about the requirements of their course in respect to dissection?

5. Is the animal house as secure as can reasonably be expected? Is its location easily deducible by intruders?

6. Can a senior member of staff with understanding of all college animal work be contacted quickly in an emergency?

Similar checklists can be written up for many cases, such as student "no platform" policies, instances of drug abuse, accidents on campus, and industrial disputes. In each case, most of the questions involve college management policy, not simply the mechanics of dealing with the media. It is little use trying to make bland statements to the press after an animal liberation break-in, if the intruders have made a video showing that the college has been causing considerable animal suffering in experiments of doubtful value. It would similarly be a waste of time, after a student riot, to face the media with articulate and well-briefed staff if they could only verify the fact that the college took no precautions against the riot, did not even know that the controversial speaker was coming, had a confused code of conduct, and possessed no effective disciplinary procedure.

It is in connection with the avoidance of PR crises that the PRP's position as a member of the college management team becomes most severely tested. Others might easily think that the college's code of conduct or safety procedures were of no concern to the PRP, and would resent recommendations from the PR office about their emendation. PRPs who suggest that admission policy should not always ignore factors such as behaviour patterns are similarly likely to be told, sharply, to mind their own business. It is such failure to realise that public relations thinking must be incorporated into all aspects of the college's management that lies behind many disasters. Time and again, analyses of such disasters show that public relations input has been excluded from an important matter of concern until everyone reads about it in their morning newspapers. Only after the excrement has hit the fan and is plastered all over the college walls are some PRPs brought in, in the forlorn hope that they can somehow clean things up before anyone notices.

Crisis prevention can often be unpopular internally. It requires focusing management's minds on aspects of the college which might merit criticism, and the PRP can so easily come to look like the college Cassandra. Conflicts, and potential conflicts, have to be examined, not swept under the carpet. Are safety regulations being ignored, because of cost and sloth? This is a potential PR timebomb. Is redundancy on the horizon, yet no-one in authority wants to discuss it? Senior management must be persuaded that this is an important public relations issue if they are not to be faced with a demoralised, hostile workforce. Is the misbehaviour of a small group of students antagonising college neighbours? This is a problem for the college to solve, not to ignore, or community relations will be impaired.

All this may not be the nicer side of PR work: it is always more pleasant to be able to concentrate on college success stories. Sound public relations must, however, be based on facts, not illusions. Real public relations work, based on genuine concern for public opinion and the public interest, is an important catalyst leading to higher standards of management.

Summary
The development of management by anticipation within public relations has increased the attention paid to issue and crisis management. Issue management involves monitoring the various trends and other factors which can affect the organisation, so that opportunities are not missed and adverse developments do not take the organisation unawares. Crisis management, though often thought of as the art of dealing with a crisis once it has struck, is more beneficially perceived as the art of preparing

the organisation in advance for the various things that can go wrong. Contingency planning can ensure that the college behaves responsibly in times of crisis, and minimises the damage to its public relations. In many cases, forward planning can also prevent public relations problems from arising.

Chapter 12. The Future of PR in Higher Education

Although public relations in Britain established itself more than 40 years ago, it has for most of that time been regarded as a profession whose time was yet to come. In recent years it seems that its time really has arrived. PR is now big business and is growing even more. The 100 largest British PR consultancies had a combined turnover of well over £100 million in 1987 (Shandwick[31] alone had billings of £26 million) and the total value of British in-house and consultancy work was probably four times as great. There are enough employees in the profession to support a specialist newspaper, *PR Week*, which has clearly prospered since its introduction as a rather thin and tentative publication in late 1984. Perhaps the most graphic illustration of the buoyancy of the profession, though, is provided by the large number of PR job advertisements in each Monday's *Guardian*.

The future of the PR industry also seems assured. A compound growth of over 35% a year throughout the 1980s has shown no sign of abating – the reported figure for 1987 was in fact 37%.[32] Few industry analysts doubt that at least one British PR company will have annual billings of over £100 million by the end of the eighties. Within higher education, too, signs have been equally positive. The university information officers' group (SCUIO) increased its membership steadily throughout the decade, and in early 1987 listed 114 members, while the polytechnic information officers' group (PPRISC) saw average attendances increase by 35% in the period 1982–1987. PR departments in colleges have been set up or strengthened, and even CVCP and CDP have made public relations appointments. This present publication – the first of its kind – is itself a symptom of the growing confidence of PR in the higher educational world.

The future brings a number of known challenges to public relations practitioners in higher education. One clear challenge, it has to be admitted, is to raise the standards of everyday practice, so that ineptitude in PR becomes very much the exception instead of commonplace. Another clear challenge is to incorporate PR consciousness in all levels of senior management. Both these topics have been covered extensively in earlier chapters of this book. There is one further known challenge for PRPs in the future which has not been covered previously, however, and this forms the topic for the remainder of this chapter.

PR and the new technologies

The information technology revolution is basically about communications. So is much of public relations. New hardware and software allow huge improvements in the collection, storing, analysis, presentation, and transmission of information, all of which must be meat and drink to the PRP. The opportunities for improvements in public relations practice are thus great indeed, and the following sections will offer a review of the various possibilities. Warning must be given of two pitfalls. The first is the danger of over-enthusiasm. It is remarkably easy to turn into a zealot for all things computerate, to divert funds into the purchase of hardware, software, and related services, and then to spend most of one's time as a terminal junkie. A small child once said "Daddy, do you get to play with toys when you've grown up?" If that child had seen a number of us at our terminals, he might well have concluded that these were indeed grown-up toys: and he might well have been right.

There is, of course, nothing the matter with enjoying one's work, but it is essential to treat the new technologies as tools to meet specific objectives, not ends in themselves. There are two tests to apply. The first is whether the new machines and software will do the existing jobs more effectively; the second is whether they are likely to enable new jobs to be done which were previously impossible. Both of these challenges are ones which exercise the minds of pro-active PRPs, helping them to stay at the leading edge of the profession.

Computer techniques will often prove better, cheaper or easier than older ones but this is not always the case. A great deal of time and money has been spent in the past, for instance, on some videotex systems which, when usage rates were analysed, proved to be less cost-effective by a factor of thousands than printed publications. However mind-boggling the potential of a new technique, the hard question that often has to be faced is: has it yet become sufficiently cost-effective to deserve a higher claim on funds than techniques shown, through the years, to have worked?

The second main pitfall to avoid is becoming so overwhelmed by all the options that a retreat to pen and paper seems the only practical solution. Anyone contemplating buying a personal computer with just two software packages, for instance — a wordprocessor and a database system — is likely to find that if the systems are to be used to the full, well over a thousand pages of complex instructions have to be mastered: and this would only be the start. Thousands more pages would have to be read to expand the system, before mastery could be gained of electronic mail, spreadsheets, page-layout packages, management analysis software, and suchlike. It cannot be too surprising that any individual wary of computers in the first place (and certainly not everyone finds them fun) is likely to decide that computers should be left to computer experts or the younger generation. Regrettably, PRPs of this viewpoint will gradually become less and less able to cope with their tasks. If they are close to retirement, retraining may not be justified, but otherwise their superiors must ensure that both encouragement and time are made available to master the new techniques. It will need to be an ongoing commitment: there is a great deal to be learned.

Quality of presentation
One of the most rewarding items of new technology for PRPs is the wordprocessor. PRPs are, for much of their time, wordsmiths, needing to produce reports, articles, leaflets, advertising copy, press releases, and correspondence, both speedily and to the highest standards. In this situation, wordprocessors — employed directly by both the PRP and the PRP's secretary — are a dream come true. In less than the time taken to write a rough draft by hand, a polished final copy can be prepared. Ideas organisers[33] can be used to prepare the first draft, segments can be moved around at will, additions and amendments can be made painlessly, and spellcheckers[34] and stylecheckers[35] can keep an eye on technical quality. Even a built-in thesaurus is provided with the latest software packages for those seeking exactly the right word. A huge increase in productivity is made possible as is a comparable increase in quality. The report that includes an error does not have to be retyped or coated in opaquing fluid; a revised version takes only moments to prepare. Last-minute corrections to mild solecisms are not avoided for fear of fraying the typist's (or one's own) nerves: indeed, very late revisions to include adjectives with more verve, or a simile with extra flair, present no difficulties at all.

Wordprocessors are also highly effective where there is a need to send letters to a large number of individuals. Sticky labels can be readily printed from databases, or letters can be "mailmerged" in a manner which allows each to be personalised. Mailmerging allows scores of letters to be sent out very fast, each appearing fully individualised: modern techniques have gone far beyond the laughably crude commercial mailshots of the seventies. The combination of carefully prepared address records and mailmerge programmes in fact allows some highly effective, fully focused communication, far removed from the scatter-gun mailings which were the best that could be achieved in the days of typewriter-and-photocopier technology.

The visual quality of materials produced by the wordprocessor can increase dramatically in other respects, particularly if one of the new laserprinters is employed. Such devices produce, at fairly modest cost, print which will look to a layman exactly like the products of traditional typesetting, and reports and press releases can be issued with an aura of great professionalism. In fact some PRPs have been so impressed with the results that they have largely forsaken traditional typesetting techniques and moved into the world of desk-top publishing.

Through page-layout software for text, and digitizers for graphics, it is certainly possible to produce in-house leaflets, newsletters, and other publications with complete control over the product, and at low cost. This is clearly a development to be watched closely, though at the present state of the technology, the authors are unable to recommend it with complete conviction. Laserprinters currently achieve a resolution of 300 dots to the linear inch, whereas "proper" typesetting systems, such as the Monotype Lasercomp, have a resolution of 2,900 dots per inch. Though the products of laserprinters are a great deal better than those of typewriters, they are still significantly below the level of traditional typesetting, and even the rumoured new generation of laserprinters, with a resolution of 600 dots per inch, should produce print quality significantly below that of traditional methods. It would at this moment be a backward step to forsake traditional typesetting completely in favour of desktop publishing.

The alert PRP can, nevertheless, gain the best of both worlds, even at the present state of the technology. This book, for instance, was produced initially on a pair of wordprocessors, and printed out for checking on a laserprinter. Once the final text was agreed, after many easily produced redrafts, typesetting command codes were added, the files were copied onto a floppy disk, and the disk was sent away to a typesetter: this allowed the expensive process of keying-in at the typesetters to be by-passed, saving most of the cost.

Universities and polytechnics which are on-line to JANET (the Joint

Academic NETwork) need not even bother to send disks away for such processing: data can be transmitted via the network to Oxford University's Monotype Lasercomp; bromides of the very highest quality are then received via the post within a few days. Another alternative is to arrange typesetting via Microlink (see below) and commercial companies such as Wordstream, which produced this text. All these methods allow the highest quality to be obtainable at a price far below that of manual typesetting. This book, indeed, is a clear example of a product that would have been financially untenable if traditional typesetting methods had been employed.

New technologies give a number of other interesting ways to improve a college's visual material. Highly professional overhead slides, for instance, can be made quickly and directly by placing acetates rather than paper in laserprinters; when business graphics software is employed in addition, the final product can be very impressive indeed. In the few weeks prior to completion of this chapter, however, it appeared that even the laserprinter-and-acetate technique might soon be old hat. A new Kodak overhead projection device, linked to a wordprocessor, allows direct projection on a screen of anything in the wordprocessor's files.

On-line information bases
About a decade ago it was being argued that teletext services would swiftly undermine the publishing business. The whole process of cutting down forests and redistributing them inked and bound was to be replaced by tapping giant electronic information banks. The precise, up-to-date information was to become available instantly on one's video screen.

Things have not quite developed as expected. Some of the limitations were made obvious by the free Oracle and Ceefax[36] services provided by ITV and BBC. This approach to mass communication is certainly capable of transmitting the latest information, but can only convey small amounts of data in a given time − far more can be gleaned in a few minutes from a newspaper than from an hour's screen-watching. Ceefax and Oracle watchers are constantly reminded that newspapers, magazines and books remain a highly effective means of transmitting information.

It is true, of course, that Ceefax and Oracle are very simple systems: a far more flexible approach is made possible by connecting an office or home computer to a central database via the telephone. All that is needed by the user is the appropriate software and a "modem", i.e. a device which converts electronic data into patterns of sound.

The dominant British viewdata service is Prestel, which claims to be the largest such service in the world. At the time of writing it offers around 300,000 pages of information, a reasonable number of which are of use to higher education. PICKUP[37] provides basic details of 6,000 short courses, MARIS[38] offers a database of information for self-study and other training materials, and SIGNPOST provides information on 300 careers. POLYTEL has since 1985 provided current vacancy information on courses at polytechnics which − and this is where the system shines − is updated daily in August and September. A similar service is to be available from UCCA, beginning in 1987, while ECCTIS[39] provides comprehensive vacancy information for the whole of higher education, including the CIHEs, along with course details on both higher and further education.

This is all impressive and indeed the usage rates of vacancy databases is getting to be quite high. ECCTIS anticipated 80,000 on-line enquiries in August and September of 1988. Nevertheless, instead of turning into a mass communication medium, as intended, Prestel had after almost a decade of development still attracted only 70−80,000 customers, and had settled down into a service used mostly by the business community. The system has been valued as a provider of information that is updated regularly, but the time and cost involved in accessing data have left Prestel relatively uncompetitive for the dissemination of slowly changing information.

By contrast with the limited uptake of Prestel, France has taken to its Teletel system in a big way. Anyone with a telephone can obtain a basic keyboard and screen (called Minitel), usually free of charge, from the Ministry of Post and Telecommunications. Officials predicted that over three million users would have them by the end of 1987. Through Minitel a whole new network of personal communication has been set up and the telephone lines are kept busy with videotex messages about goods and services for sale, all kinds of advice, games, and even dating facilities, as well as the telephone directory which was the impetus for installing the system in the first place.

The main lesson learned by experience of teletext and videotex so far is that they do not simply replace existing systems; they do not just allow us to do the same things as publishing but in different ways. Rather they allow us to do things which previously were not feasible. Each communication system has its strengths, weaknesses, and opportunities, and the PRP must be sure to understand them, and be ready to exploit the opportunities as they arise.

One of the most interesting derivations of central database systems involves capturing huge amounts of data (up to 600 megabytes) on a "CD-ROM"[40] − which looks to the uninitiated exactly like a domestic compact disk. ECCTIS is one of the leaders in using this technology.

ECTTIS's Prestel database covers the basic details of 40,000 HE and FE courses, as well as vacancy details on higher education courses, but accessing this information through the telephone wires is slow and fairly expensive. By transferring the information onto a compact disk, users with the necessary equipment can access the information far more speedily, and without incurring any of Prestel's telephone charges. This system is certainly impressive to use: in fact, the whole ECCTIS database, along with associated databases such as that of PICKUP, can be carried on 20% of the disk's capacity, so future disks are expected to include additional databases, such as those of MARIS.

The CD-ROM might seem to be at home mostly in conveying very large quantities of static information: indeed, encyclopaedias are now appearing on the medium. The system can, however, allow for updates. The ECCTIS CD-ROM will be kept current by issuing revised versions to subscribers every three months (the disk itself costs little), while more frequent updates will be achievable through a "softstrip". A softstrip is a half-inch wide printed bar, roughly analogous to a bar code, and holding up to 5,500 bytes of information. This strip is read by an optical scanning device onto a hard disk which complements the CD-ROM, making it appear to the user as though the compact disk has itself been updated. The softstrip will, in fact, allow ECCTIS to update its current vacancy information daily during the August-September rush, either by sending copies of the softstrip through the post, or by publication in a national newspaper.

The ECCTIS CD-ROM system should shortly revolutionise the process by which careers advisers give information to enquirers about higher education, and undoubtedly other uses will be found for the technology. Where the information involved is less immense, floppy disks can be a convenient medium. *PR Planner*, for instance, which provides brief details of around 10,000 publications and broadcasting programmes, is now available on floppy disk; this allows, amongst other things, swift print-out of address labels appropriate to the topic of any individual press release. Until on-line provision of data dramatically improves, it is likely that more and more information will be available in disk form. PRPs will progressively need to be able both to use, and to provide, information in this format.

Departmental databases

PRPs often have to provide accurate up-to-date information at the drop of a hat, for instance in response to enquiries from MPs or journalists. Modern technology is ideal for storing and presenting such information. Statistics, policy decisions and other data can be fed into a computer on a daily basis and then be instantly available on a workstation screen while the PRP is still speaking on the telephone. By 1990 it should be commonplace for all PR departments – even those that can afford only a single domestic-type microcomputer – to have their most-needed information stored electronically.

Electronic communications

Electronic mail systems have now been set up within a number of colleges. Instead of sending memoranda on paper, internal messages are sent via the main computer network, and picked up at other work-stations. The process is very fast, and brings with it several additional advantages: the receipt of messages, for instance, can be electronically logged, doing away with uncertainties about the postal system and all those claims that one's message has never been received.

External communication systems are an extension of the internal mailing idea. The best-known version in the UK, Telecom Gold, started off purely as an electronic mailbox, permitting subscribers to send one another messages and documents more reliably, and faster, than through the post. It now has additional features, such as radiopaging when an express message is received in one's mailbox, and the ability to send messages to subscribers of other systems all over the world.

An offshoot of Telecom Gold, providing a kind of halfway house between traditional methods and electronic mail, is the Microlink service, which allows, amongst other things, swift communications with non-subscribers. Letters are typed up in the usual way on the wordprocessor, but instead of being printed out and posted, they are sent via Telecom Gold and Microlink: the letters are then printed out on a machine at the Post Office delivery office nearest the recipient's address. Any letter transmitted before 8.00 pm will be delivered in the following morning's post in a "telemessage" envelope, providing an impact similar to that of the now-defunct telegram service. One-to-One, the main competitor to Telecom Gold, offers a courier service based on the same idea, but guaranteeing delivery anywhere in the UK within 2 hours.

A rather older technology is telex, which has allowed swift communication between any of the 150,000 telex machines in Britain (and 2 million world-wide), but at fairly high cost. Dedicated telex machines and telephone lines are necessary for the usual service, and the cost of this has often been considered too high for colleges. Now, however, it is possible to tap into the telex network with an ordinary micro and modem via Microlink, allowing use of the service at a cost which any PRP can justify. Unfortunately, the same is not yet true of facsimile transmission ("fax"), which allows transmission via the telephone of pictures, drawings, diagrams, and symbols, as well as text. This system has been in existence for many years, and though it has been growing steadily cheaper, dedicated equipment is still required, which might not be justifiable for occasional use.†

A development worth mentioning in this section is the electronic noticeboard. Many colleges have acquired an internal viewdata system which allows information to be shown on monitors around the campus. Such systems, though often useful, have suffered from their low visual impact: the monitors are of the size of normal television screens, and thus do not catch the attention of crowds of people on the move. Electronic noticeboards get round this problem, flashing messages in letters several inches high on screens which are typically four or eight feet long. A number of visual tricks can be used to ensure that the messages are noticed, such as flashing, scrolling, rolling from the centre, and rippling. The noticeboards can be used singly, and "programmed" in situ, or a number can be placed in strategic points around the campus and controlled centrally from a single microprocessor. Used imaginatively such devices can make a considerable contribution to internal communications.

Aids to mobility

Many developments of the new technologies not mentioned above – electronic diaries, spreadsheets, budgetary control and critical path software, for example – will be of distinct interest to PRPs in their administrative and managerial roles. Because much public relations work is focused on deadlines, PRPs should be able to argue a better case for such aids than many of their colleagues. As professional communicators, also, they may justify purchase of the various new communication aids made possible by cellular networks. Pocket telephones, for instance, will shortly cease to be the status symbols of the wealthy, and will help maintain the accessibility which is so important to sound public relations work.

Lap-top computers, too, will shortly become the norm. Such devices, which can be carried around wherever the job takes one, allow notes, memoranda, reports, press releases, etc to be prepared very speedily,

---

†The world of IT moves fast! Just as this book was about to be printed reports were received of a new system which will allow any IBM PC or clone to be used as a facsimile machine. By the addition of an expansion card, the PC can be used as a fax receiver; images received can be enlarged, reduced, rotated, and printed out on a dot-matrix or laser printer. With the addition of a scanner, the PC can also be used to transmit fax images. The system is significantly cheaper than any existing fax machine, allows the PC to be switched between fax and other roles at will, and does not require a dedicated telephone line.

and downloaded into one's workstation on return to the office or transmitted instantly via an "acoustic coupler" and an ordinary telephone. They are coming to be standard tools of journalists, who can join a conference, type a report while the guests are speaking, and transmit a revised version during the breaks. When combined with cellular networks, it is not even necessary to find a telephone: the report can be transmitted instantly from virtually anywhere. The PRP who has not learned to type, and knows nothing of baud rates or ASCII codes, will be at an acute disadvantage once techniques as powerful as this are more commonplace and readily affordable.

Conclusion

This chapter has given only a brief review of the opportunities made available to the public relations profession by the information technology revolution. Many other opportunities exist or will shortly be appearing. For instance, direct broadcasting and narrowcasting by satellite and cable will shortly create considerable demand for video material. Even more opportunities will be provided by electronic stills photography, which will allow cameras to capture pictures on magnetic disk, and images to be transmitted instantly by the telephone, with no pause for chemical processing. Such developments exemplify the ever-changing nature of the communications world in which PRPs operate.

Practitioners of any age or length of experience who think that their learning days are behind them are not the ones who will serve their college best in the future. Nor should they just wait until the new techniques are fully developed elsewhere. The ethos of research and new knowledge which characterises colleges should encourage PRPs to experiment and be at the forefront of their profession.

Summary

PR is a growth industry, and already big business. One of the main challenges to PRPs in higher education is to ensure that the increased professionalism of public relations in the business world is at least mirrored within their own sphere. An immediate challenge for individual PRPs is to master the many new communications techniques made available through the information technology revolution. Great increases in productivity, in quality of work, and in creative thinking, can be achieved by those fully conversant with: wordprocessing, mail-merging, database management, desk-top publishing, laserprinters, business graphics software, on-line and off-line information bases, electronic mail, electronic noticeboards, cellular network communications, and lap-top computers − but considerable time, commitment, and support from the college, will be necessary if the PRP is to keep pace fully with developments.

Appendix 1. Public Relations and Marketing

In academic circles over recent years, PR has often been represented as marketing under another name, or at least as a specialist branch of marketing. The main reason for this may have been the growing academic respectability, and credibility, of marketing theory, combined with the absence from higher education of PR as an intellectual discipline. Marketing theorists, like theorists in all intellectual disciplines, tend to be imperialist, seeing the problems of others as ripe for interpretation through their own set of paradigms and methodologies. Some have even gone so far as to relabel PR as "social marketing", a move which, if not resisted, could cement its sub-categorisation. Academics are not alone, either, in attempting to subsume public relations within marketing. Many marketing practitioners have a limited understanding of PR, seeing it only in terms of "free" publicity and other forms of promotion which exist just to stimulate sales.

The practical reality, however, is that marketing and public relations personnel share some objectives and methods, and play interrelated roles in their organisations, and yet pursue overall goals which are fundamentally different. They are guided by quite distinct views of what matters. The formal definitions of the two subjects should make this clear. The "official" definition of public relations formulated by the IPR, as we saw in Chapter 1, is "the deliberate, planned and sustained effort to establish and maintain mutual understanding between an organisation and its public." The Institute of Marketing, on the other hand, defines its subject as "the management function responsible for identifying, anticipating and satisfying customer requirements at a profit."

The two definitions clearly refer to different functions, with different objectives. Success to the marketeer is measured in terms of more widespread, more profitable sales: the reputation of the organisation only enters into consideration to the extent to which it aids or hinders that goal (though the sound marketing officer will be well aware of the value of good public relations in developing "leads" and retaining consumer loyalty). For the marketing manager the only really important public is the customer. Success to the public relations officer, however, is measured not in terms that accountants find so dear to their hearts, but in terms of increasing the mutual understanding and respect between the organisation and many different audiences, including a number which have nothing to do with "sales". This goal may seem less financially beneficial in the short term, but it is crucial to the organisation's development and long-term survival.

Since PRPs work on a very broad canvas, involving themselves to some extent in every facet of their organisations' operations, their work inevitably at times goes in tandem with the marketeers'. The two managers at such times have much in common. An organisation that achieves a good reputation is generally one that will also achieve good sales. The marketeer can benefit from the work of the PRP. Likewise, whatever happens in the sales arena will spill over into the organisation's general profile. A company that treats its customers shabbily will quickly acquire a bad reputation which will affect its other operations such as recruitment, labour negotiations or raising of capital. A company with a good customer relationship, however, will benefit in its other areas.

There is much to be gained, therefore, by ensuring that an organisation's marketing policy is in harmony with its public relations policy, and the PRP and marketeer will frequently find themselves in close contact. They will have a mutual interest in various techniques, and will be natural allies over matters such as survey methods, external presentation of the organisation's strengths, and corporate advertising. Their professional interests will nevertheless differ significantly. Though the public relations practitioner will know about marketing mix, product life cycles, market segmentation, the Boston Matrix, and suchlike, these will be much closer to the centre of the marketeer's world. The marketeer, on the other hand, will be a lot less interested in matters close to the PRP's heart, such as the techniques of internal communication, relations with the local community, the needs of various editors, the prioritisation of target audiences, and the means by which opinion-leaders and decision makers can be reached.

Though it is an item for controversy, we would argue that the "public relations perspective" is usually more appropriate to senior managers of a college than the "marketing perspective" *except* in such areas as specialist short courses and income-generation activities like the summer letting of accommodation. In recent years there has been much governmental pressure on colleges to manage their resources more effectively. Considering the large amount of taxpayers' money that supports education this is not an unreasonable demand, and marketing of income-generating activities should thus be as fully professional as possible. However, income generation must for most colleges remain a secondary activity: their primary purpose is to provide an educational service for society. If a college inverts this perspective and runs itself essentially as a "market led" profit-making business, then there is a serious likelihood that it will lose sight of its social mission. Courses will be mounted solely on the basis of their financial viability; student support services will be trimmed to the minimum; student/staff ratios will be reduced. All this may make economic sense but poor educational sense. Principals who are attracted predominantly to the marketing approach should ask themselves whether they see their roles as managing directors or as academic leaders.

It is true that the cost-effective matching of demand to supply remains of considerable significance even where the college's standard offering – the long course – is concerned, but this should not lead to excessive concentration on "sales" to the potential customer. For long courses the provider of payment is very rarely the consumer of the service; decisions to resource the course are taken on broad educational need and national policy rather than its capacity to attract applicants. In this situation, "identifying, anticipating and satisfying customer requirements" is less appropriate than being attuned to, and being seen to be attuned to, the broad educational needs of society.

The attempted subsumption of PR within marketing, as noted above, results largely from the greater development of marketing as an academic discipline. Degree-level courses on marketing have been abundant, and thus those interested in the general PR/advertising/marketing area have nearly always been directed into an academic study of the latter, and have come to interpret PR within the *weltanschauung* of marketing. But currently, the claims of public relations to be treated as a separate degree-level subject are being recognised, and appropriate methodologies and paradigms are being developed which substantiate its separate identity. Appendix 7 pursues this theme.

Appendix 2. The Ethical Dimension

Insofar as public relations deals with issues like truth, confidentiality, honesty, advocacy, public interest, employer's interest, and reputation, it is a business that has a significant ethical dimension. Practitioners who aspire to do their job professionally have to conform to high personal standards. When the Institute of Public Relations was founded in 1948, the setting of a code of conduct was one of its earliest tasks, and the code (see Appendix 3) has been subject to constant scrutiny and revision ever since.

Many public relations practitioners will have undergone no previous apprenticeship, but will have had to learn for themselves the nature of their work. Some have thus started with ethical qualms about their duties, imagining perhaps that the job might involve adding a gloss to the truth on some occasions, while on others using guile to keep outsiders from scenting discreditable facts. Few newcomers suppose that they will be expected actually to lie for their living, and yet it tends to be supposed that a series of clever half-truths will be required of them if they are to earn their keep. While a diplomat is said to be a gentleman who lies for his country, so PRPs are imagined by some to be professional communicators who merely dissemble for their employers.

As the newcomers learn to be effective in their tasks, though, it starts to become clear that most of the anticipated ethical problems do not arise. In providing material for various publications, for example, it soon sinks in that prose which is overloaded with panegyrics and focuses on emotion, and completely ignores anything unfavourable, simply does not work in public relations contexts. In the college context, prospectuses which aim primarily at *persuading* rather than *informing* do considerable harm to the college's academic credibility. Press releases which read as "puffs" are immediately ignored: editors want solid facts, without any of the dressing. If the very first sentences of the release, in fact, leave out any of the "six W's" — the what, where, when, who, why and how of the story — in favour of empty panegyrics, then the release goes straight in the bin.

Though media relations is only one aspect of public relations, PR newcomers tend to suppose that it will be this aspect of their work which will lead to most ethical difficulties. Relationships with journalists, in fact, soon prove to lack most of the anticipated ethical tensions. The paradigm relationship certainly does not involve the journalist probing away for facts that might be used in a damaging fashion, with the PRP weighing each word carefully to see that nothing is given away. In reality, good PRPs and journalists are allies, the latter gaining a useful source of information, and the former — with just a few exceptions —

being provided with highly desirable publicity. Working relations are thus built up by being genuinely useful to the representatives of the media: and this involves being honest sources of information. Journalists can ask plenty of other people in the organisation for information — the union leaders, known activists, or members of boards recognised to be "leaky" — and will only continue to deal with the PRP if this makes their work easier and provides more reliable information. The PRP that constantly evades difficult questions, tries to "flannel", or is convicted of half-truths, just will not be dealt with again.

Once they begin to form working relationships with the media, newcomers are sometimes asked to engage in a specific area of ethically dubious practice: to "use their influence with the press" to get a legitimate story spiked. In those early, naive, days, one of the tasks of a PRP might be thought to be manipulating the press in the way desired by senior management. It soon emerges, however, that though in certain circumstances such things *can* be done, they will be done only at great cost to the long-term effectiveness of the PR office. All the capital built up with an editor or journalist will be burnt in one go if a story has to be spiked through special pleading: and the capital is just too important to be wasted. PRPs need the editors and journalists to welcome their material; to be open to suggestions for features; to be willing to follow up apparently dull leads on the PRP's recommendation: and the type of working relationship leading to this is simply not compatible with attempts to manipulate.

In general, the communications process will only be effective if it is open and honourable; this is true not just of media relations but of all aspects of PR. If dubious tactics are used in any "lobbying", then serious long-term damage can be caused. If the internal newsletter focuses on the principal's statements and the cheesecake and ignores anything contentious, it will be seen as an "organ of management" and won't be read. If supposedly informative publications reek of perfume, then everyone suspects that the smell of rat is being disguised. Dubious ethical practices are always likely to undermine the esteem in which an organisation is held: to engage in them, on the assumption that they will *improve* the organisation's public relations, represents essentially confused thinking.

As the new public relations practitioner really comes to understand the role, then, it will be discovered that the needs of the task push in the direction of ethical behaviour, not away from it. This leads many of the initial qualms about the post to disappear. It will also be found that there is surprisingly little pressure from inside the organisation to act in an unethical manner. Where such pressure exists, it usually results from naivety, based on the assumption that public relations practitioners possess arcane means of secretly manipulating audiences. There are no such arcane means. The PRP cannot "get at" people to make them think that night is day. If the organisation's actions merit public displeasure, there is very little that public relations activity can do to cover it up, whatever the budget or talent available; similarly, if the organisation does not have good things to tell the outside world, the PRP cannot manufacture them. PRPs for organisations which do not *deserve* public support have an ultimately hopeless task: none of the seeds they plant will grow. Once all this is understood by the developing public relations practitioner, the main response to those who ask for manipulative activity is simply to point out the facts about what can be achieved. If this doesn't work immediately, and the senior member of staff continues to press for dubious actions, the request can be deflected with the assertion "I'm sorry, I can't do that: it's against the IPR professional code of practice." This assertion, unlike "I'm sorry, I think it will do us long-term harm", or "I'm sorry, but I don't think it is ethical", allows no comeback even by the most senior and insensitive.

A reader might here begin to think that this flow of argument is all too smooth. The view that enlightened self-interest pushes the PR profession inexorably towards the ethical, and that pressures to be unethical are few and easily overcome, might seem too glib. The suspicion might even be aroused in the reader that "a PR job" is being done on PR. Surely there must be some ethical tensions somewhere?

It has to be admitted that the detractors of the public relations profession would score points if they referred to the fact that practitioners inevitably broadcast only the rosier side of their organisations: the successes and efficiency, but not the failures and incompetence. The PR office, undoubtedly, does not treat all facts about the organisation in the same manner. Information which can be used to the organisation's credit will be tracked down and made much of publicly whereas the same cannot be said of unflattering data. Where college personnel are highly effective, for instance, the PR office will find ways of transmitting the fact widely; where college personnel are incompetent, the fact will not be broadcast to the public, though it might arguably be in the public's interest to do so.

Selectivity of information for external presentation can undoubtedly cause some problems for a PRP. To take a true example from college life, each year some academic departments seek to counter damaging evidence of their subject's bad employability record by asking the public relations office to make use of carefully selected employment information. Such information will be entirely accurate, so far as it goes, and yet its unqualified use could mislead potential applicants about their job prospects. The experienced PRP will resist using such material, largely because it is unethical, clearly violating the IPR code of practice, but also because it offends against the college's long-term interests. The college that is seen to be entirely honest on such issues, and capable of facing up to its problems, proves itself thereby to be mature, confident, and worthy of a good name. The under-recruiting department, of course, will not be convinced by this, but the PRP can stand firm, insisting that the interests of the college as a whole must come first.

There are other cases of selective information use, though, where the PRP finds it harder to argue that enlightened self-interest is consistent with a high moral stance. Take the case of the department with a bad research and consultancy record that eventually makes progress in these areas. Seen from a neutral viewpoint, the situation could be described in terms of a department which was once awful at research and consultancy becoming average. The story transmitted via the PR office could never-theless be: "300% Increase in Research and Consultancy Funding for Dept X ... Largest Individual Award Received by Dept for 20 Years ... Principal Praises Department's New Spirit of Achievement". Enthusiastic support of this kind would certainly be expected of the college PR office; a purely dispassionate approach, leading to damning by faint praise, would be wholly out of character for any real-life PR team.

Transmitting publicly a sympathetic, rather than neutral, view of the organisation's activities comes naturally to the PR office, which will be, by nature, an enthusiast for the organisation it serves. The office will always treat the organisation's setbacks with greater public sympathy than a neutral observer, and will always be encouraging, publicly, about quite small achievements.

Sceptics about public relations practice might seem to have found something damaging about the profession here, and yet there is in truth something rather silly about expecting the PR office to act without an inbuilt sympathy for its employing organisation. All good employees would be expected to take a sympathetic view of their organisation's activities – such loyalty is a virtue, not a vice – and certainly nobody would expect PRPs to act publicly as disinterested third parties; part of their job, indeed, is to act as advocates of the organisation, seeing that its case is made in as coherent and persuasive a way as possible. Acting thus is not ethically unsound; listeners will know that the case being presented is that of the organisation, not that of an independent arbiter. The ethical analogy is that of a barrister arguing his client's case.

Real ethical difficulties for PRPs only come when they are in danger of moving beyond the realm of sympathetic exposition – which is perfectly legitimate – to the misleading, which must offend against their professional code of practice and against normal moral principles. Distinguishing between sympathetic exposition and the misleading certainly remains a problem, but practitioners should not think that the nature of their work inevitably pushes them towards fudging and down the slippery slope to the unethical. It does not, though vigilance is essential.

The sceptic about PR activity might correctly identify cases of individual malpractice through dubious use of selective information, but would not be able to claim that PR *per se* is compromised. A last attempt could nevertheless be made to show that in a subtle way, PR practice is contrary to the public good. Individual PR officers, it could be argued, might be able to remain honourable in presenting to the public a sympathetic view of their organisation, and yet there is an army of such people at work: perhaps 20,000 in Britain alone. With such a number of professional enthusiasts and apologists at work, opponents could claim, much inefficiency will be excused, much that is indifferent will be praised, and the spur to improve will be blunted: the overall effect of the work of the profession could thus be socially damaging.

This would be a very good attack on the PR profession were it not for the fact that it leaves out one entire side of the PRP's function. Though public relations practitioners might be highly sympathetic to the organisation's foibles in public, the "spokesman" role is only part of their function. One of the most important elements of sound PR practice, as noted in Chapter 1, involves acting as the organisation's conscience – acting behind the scenes to ensure that the organisation *deserves* sound public relations.

Effective public relations practice, as we have seen, must involve listening to the audiences, and seeing that appropriate internal action is taken whenever the organisation merits censure. No PRP will be able to "smooth things over" for long when legitimate complaints can be brought against the organisation; the only practicable way forward is to make sure that the offending actions are changed. PRPs need to act as goads ensuring that such changes are made, because if changes are not made, the organisation's public relations can never be sound and the PRPs' lives are made impossible. The effective PRP will not just wait for complaints to arise, either, before recommending changes in policy or action. It will be necessary to anticipate reactions to any existing and planned activity, blowing the whistle early if it is likely that damage to the organisation's public relations will be caused.

Effective PRPs will certainly not, therefore, succour complacency internally, nor will they make it easier for damaging activities to continue, however loyal and sympathetic to foibles they may seem when speaking publicly. The overall effect of PR work, in fact – as long as it is properly carried out in the best interests of the employer – will be socially beneficial. If the 20,000 or so British PRPs carried out their jobs really well, they would, far from being defenders of complacency and incompetence, be one of the most powerful forces ensuring that the employers' actions *merited* the esteem of the public.

Appendix 3. Code of Professional Conduct of the Institute of Public Relations

The IPR's code, revised in 1986, defines high personal standards of public relations conduct and practice. All applicants for membership to the Institute agree to be bound by it and there is a professional practices committee which considers complaints against members who are said to breach the code. The Council is empowered to suspend members or terminate their membership for professional misconduct.

1. **Standards of professional conduct**
   A member shall have a positive duty to observe the highest standards in the practice of public relations. Furthermore a member has the personal responsibility at all times to deal fairly and honestly with his client, employer or employees, past or present, with fellow members, with the media of communication, and above all else with the public.

2. **Media of communication**
   A member shall not engage in any practice which tends to corrupt the integrity of the media of communication.

3. **Undisclosed interests**
   A member shall have the duty to ensure that the actual interest of any organisation with which he may be professionally concerned is adequately declared.

4. **Rewards to holders of public office**
   A member shall not, with intent to further his interests (or those of his client or employer), offer or give any reward to a person holding public office if such action is inconsistent with the public interest.

5. **Dissemination of information** A member shall have a positive duty at all times to respect the truth and in this regard not to disseminate false or misleading information knowingly or recklessly and to use proper care to avoid doing so inadvertently.

6. **Confidential information**
   A member shall not disclose (except upon the order of a court of competent jurisdiction) or make use of information given or obtained in confidence from his employer, or client, past or present, for personal gain or otherwise.

7. **Conflicts of interest**
   A member shall not represent conflicting interests but may rep-

resent competing interests with the express consent of the parties concerned.

8. **Disclosure of beneficial financial interests**
   A member with a beneficial financial interest in or from an organisation shall not recommend the use of that organisation, nor make use of its services on behalf of his client or employer, without declaring his interest.

9. **Payment contingent upon achievements**
   A member shall not negotiate or agree terms with a prospective employer or client on the basis of payment contingent upon specific future public relations achievements.

10. **Employment of holders of public office**
    A member who employs or is responsible for employing or recruiting a member of either House of Parliament, a member of the European Parliament or a person elected to public office, whether in a consultative or executive capacity, shall disclose this fact and also the object and nature of the employment to the Executive Director of the Institute who shall enter it in a register kept for the purpose. A member of the Institute who himself falls into these categories shall be directly responsible for disclosing or causing to be disclosed to the Executive Director the same information as may relate to himself. (The register referred to in this clause shall be open to public inspection at the offices of the Institute during office hours.)

11. **Injury to other members**
    A member shall not maliciously injure the professional reputation of another member.

12. **Reputation of the profession**
    A member shall not conduct himself in any manner which is or is likely to be detrimental to the reputation of the Institute or the profession of public relations.

13. **Upholding the code**
    A member shall uphold the code, shall co-operate with fellow members in so doing and in enforcing decisions on any matter arising from its application. If a member has reason to believe that another member has been engaged in practices which may be in breach of this code, it shall be his duty first to inform the member concerned and then to inform the Institute if these practices do not cease. It is the duty of all members to assist the Institute to implement this code, and the Institute will support any member so doing.

14. **Other professions**

    A member shall, when working in association with other professionals, respect the codes of other professions and shall not knowingly be party to any breach of such codes.

15. **Professional updating**

    A member shall be expected to be aware of and observe this code, any amendments to it and any other codes which shall be incorporated in this code and to remain up-to-date with the content and recommendations of any guidance papers as may be issued by the Institute and shall have a duty to take all reasonable steps to conform to good practice as expressed in such guidance papers or practice papers.

16. **Instruction of others**

    A member shall not knowingly cause or permit another person or organisation to act in a manner inconsistent with this code or be a party to such action.

17. **Interpreting the Code**

    In the interpretation of the code, the Law of England shall apply.

Appendix 4. The g-Factor — a Numerate Approach to PR Management

John Greenall

The following, slightly edited, is a paper prepared in 1969 for private circulation and discussion. It has never previously been published but is included here to demonstrate further how quantified measures can be brought into a management art that is often thought of as operating by hunch. It will be particularly valuable to readers who have been attracted by the concepts described in Chapters 4 and 6.

Traditionally public relations managers in carrying out their programmes have limited resources of staff and money. By contrast there is an unlimited choice of activities at their disposal.

They therefore have a king-size managerial problem in deciding whether to deploy resources thinly over a wide range of activities or to concentrate them on to a selected few.

In resolving this problem they are guided mainly by experience and intuition. It is likely that public relations will always call for a large element of personal judgement, and decisions will have to be taken with fewer facts available than one would like. Nonetheless this should not be taken as an excuse for not trying to bring as much objectivity into the art as possible.

This paper attempts to rationalise some of the processes by which a PR manager constructs a programme of activities. The method does not pretend to be a foolproof formula which can be applied unthinkingly to any PR situation. Indeed its value can only be as good as the practitioner's own skill in assigning the right priorities to goals and in judging the effectiveness of each PR activity. However, it is a tool which, in its present form or with amendments, many practitioners may find useful when preparing their programme.

The problem of what to undertake is bedevilled by the fact that the benefits of any PR activities are not confined to a specific goal. For example, a works exhibition, mounted solely with the intention of informing employees about their company's products, can also be seen by customers who visit the factory and so it can also have some effect on sales which is quite a different goal. This latter effect may be negligible but can the PR manager afford to ignore it completely? How much of the effort in organising the exhibition should be devoted to its possible impact on customers?

The method described here takes account of this spill-over value and gives an indication of how much effort should be given to the pursuit of different goals.

Firstly, it is necessary to introduce two measurements which I shall call the "priority rating" and the "effectiveness rating".

The *priority rating* is a scale numbered from 1 to 10 which can be used to give relative importance to public relations goals. Thus a goal which is considered to have the highest priority will be given a rating of 10; a goal with low priority can be numbered 1. In between these extremes the other goals can be placed in order of importance according to the judgement of the practitioner. It may be that certain goals will be deemed to have equal priorities. In these cases the same priority rating is given to each.

As a simple example, suppose that a PR manager considers that there are five goals to achieve:

- to establish the reputation of the company
- to increase general knowledge about the company
- to motivate potential customers to buy the product
- to attract high-quality staff
- to maintain the loyalty of existing staff

The priority rating might therefore be applied as in Table 1.

Table 1

Goal	Priority
Establish reputation	10
Improve general knowledge	10
Increase sales	8
Recruit staff	5
Develop internal relations	2

The ratings exemplified here indicate that the PR manager considers as urgent the need to establish company reputation and to increase general knowledge; these goals figure equally with scores of 10. Assistance to the sales function is also seen as very important (8) but not quite as pressing as the first two. Staff recruitment (5) must receive some attention but internal relations (2) can almost be ignored at present.

In a PR programme, goals must be related to identified publics so a refinement of the above process is to list each principal public against each goal and then to assign priority ratings accordingly. This might be as in Table 2.

Table 2

Goal	Principal Public	Priority rating
Establish reputation	Government	8
	Top management	10
Improve general knowledge	Opinion-forming groups	10
	General public	7
	Potential customers	10
Increase sales	Existing customers	8
	Potential customers	4
Recruit staff	Experienced managers	5
	New graduates	3
	Clerical/secretarial	2
Develop internal relations	Own management	2
	Office staff	2
	Manual workers	3
Miscellaneous	Miscellaneous	5

The effectiveness rating is the next measure to introduce. This also is a scale numbered 1 to 10 but in addition it can have zero and negative values. It reflects the PR manager's judgement of how effective a PR activity (say press relations or a works visit) is likely to be when applied to a given goal.

Again, 10 is the highest rating and 1 is normally the lowest. Thus, considering the goals, publics and priorities illustrated above, a PR manager might assign the following ratings (listed in the same order as in Table 2) to the likely effectiveness of a film about the firm's products: 4, 6, 8, 5, 10, 6, 8, 7, 7, 3, 7, 9, 10, 5. (Hence a film would be judged to be twice as effective for increasing sales to existing customers − 6 − as it would for recruiting clerical staff − 3).

Similar assignments can be made for other activities and a matrix can be drawn up. A zero rating is given where an activity is likely to make no contribution towards a goal. Also negative ratings can be given to activities that will be damaging to the achievement of goals. This might occur, for instance, where a lavish party, organised as an aid to internal relations, could bring protests of extravagance from shareholders. Such a case is dealt with below.

Let us call the goals G_1, G_2, G_3 etc, the publics P_1, P_2, P_3 etc, and the activities A_1, A_2, A_3 etc.

The matrix will therefore be in the form of Table 3 where typical priority ratings have been inserted in column 3 and typical effectiveness ratings in columns 4, 5, 6 and 7 (at this stage ignore the figures in brackets).

Table 3

1	2	3	4	5	6	...	7
Goal	**Public**	**Priority**	**ACTIVITIES**				
			A_1	A_2	A_3	...	A_n
G_1	P_1	10	8(80)	4(40)	10(100)	...	−1(−10)
	P_2	4	10(40)	2 (8)	7 (28)	...	2 (8)
G_2	P_3	9	4(36)	3(27)	10 (90)	...	4 (36)
	P_1	8	6(48)	5(40)	3 (24)	...	9 (72)
G_3	P_4	3	7(21)	6(18)	1 (3)	...	7 (21)
	P_5	5	3(15)	6(30)	0 (0)	...	5 (25)
G_4	P_6	1	5 (5)	10(10)	6 (6)	...	1 (1)
	P_7	1	5 (5)	9 (9)	7 (7)	...	3 (3)
G_n	P_n	4	6(24)	5(20)	8 (32)	...	6 (24)

A few examples will make the meaning of the table clear. Activity A_3 is seen to be a very effective way of achieving goals G_1 (public P_1) and G_2 (public P_3) but is virtually useless for achieving goal G_2 (public P_1) and G_3 (public P_4). It will have no effect at all on goal G_3 (public P_5). The effectiveness rating for these examples are seen to be respectively 10, 10, 3, 1, 0.

Activity A_n is an interesting case, for although it will be effective for goal G_2/P_1 and G_3/P_4 with ratings of 9 and 7, it can have a negative (and therefore damaging) effect on goal G_1/P_1. If this activity is carried out, steps will need to be taken to prevent the damage.

Even at this stage, therefore, the goal/activity matrix is proving to be of help to the PR manager in showing that efforts will be better rewarded if each activity is confined to the solution of a limited number of goals. Table 3, for example, shows that although activity A_2 will have *some* effect on all the goals, it would be wise to concentrate this activity on the problems of goal G_4/P_6 and G_4/P_7.

But the principal value of the matrix lies in what I shall immodestly label the "g-Factor". This factor is defined as a measure which combines the likely success of a public relations activity in achieving its goal, with the priority assigned to that goal. Mathematically it is the product of the priority rating and the effectiveness rating.

High g-Factors indicate those activities which will stand a good chance of success in achieving high priority objectives. Numerically the g-Factor will normally lie between 0 and 100 inclusive although occasionally it will have a negative reading.

Table 3 shows the g-Factors in parentheses. Each one is arrived at by multiplying a *priority rating* by the appropriate *effectiveness rating*. Thus goal G_2, with public P_3 in mind, is deemed to have a priority rating 9. Activity A_1 when used to achieve this goal is considered to have an effectiveness rating 4. The g-Factor is therefore $9 \times 4 = 36$.

We are now in a position to re-arrange our g-Factors in series as in table 4.

Table 4

g-Factor	Activity	Goal	Public	Resources needed	
				Staff	**Budget**
100	A_3	G_1	P_1		
90	A_3	G_2	P_3		
80	A_1	G_1	P_1		
72	A_n	G_2	P_1		
48	A_1	G_2	P_1		
40	A_1 A_2 A_2	G_1 G_1 G_2	P_2 P_1 P_1		
etc					

This table clearly shows in descending order of importance those activities which should be built into the PR programme and also the goals to be achieved. The two columns "resources needed" are included as a reminder that no activities should be planned without a realistic allocation of time and money.

I have used the symbols G, P and A for convenience and to keep the argument in general terms. Now let us apply this method to the specific example given in table 2. There we have assumed for simplicity's sake that the PRP has only five goals plus "miscellaneous". For each goal there are two or three principal publics in view. A few of these publics are common to more than one goal. Priority ratings have already been assigned to the goal/public combinations. The next step is to construct a matrix with a range of possible activities. In practice this range would probably be quite extensive but again for simplicity I have confined it to six activities: local, national and trade press relations; corporate booklet (history, organisation, products, etc); internal company newspaper; speakers' panel. In addition there is a category "PR advice to the board and management".

Table 5 shows how a practitioner in certain circumstances might judge

Table 5

PR Goal	Principal public	Priority	Local press	National press	Trade press	Corporate booklet	Company newsletter	Speakers' panel	PR advice to board management
Establish reputation	Government	8	0 (0)	9 (72)	6 (48)	5 (40)	1 (8)	7 (56)	10 (80)
	Industrial leaders	10	2 (20)	10 (100)	8 (80)	6 (60)	2 (20)	8 (80)	10 (100)
Improve general knowledge	Opinion-forming groups	10	1 (10)	10 (100)	6 (60)	7 (70)	3 (30)	8 (80)	10 (100)
	General public	7	2 (14)	10 (70)	4 (28)	6 (42)	2 (14)	7 (49)	10 (70)
	Potential customers	10	2 (20)	7 (70)	9 (90)	8 (80)	4 (40)	9 (90)	10 (100)
Increase sales	Existing customers	8	1 (8)	6 (48)	8 (64)	6 (48)	5 (40)	5 (40)	10 (80)
	Potential customers	4	2 (8)	6 (24)	9 (36)	8 (32)	5 (20)	6 (24)	10 (40)
Recruit staff	Experienced managers	5	2 (10)	4 (20)	7 (35)	6 (30)	6 (30)	5 (25)	10 (50)
	New graduates	3	1 (3)	4 (12)	2 (6)	6 (18)	5 (15)	4 (12)	10 (30)
	Clerical/secretarial	2	8 (16)	2 (4)	1 (2)	4 (8)	8 (16)	1 (2)	10 (20)
Develop internal relations	Own management	2	5 (10)	5 (10)	2 (4)	3 (6)	8 (16)	2 (4)	10 (20)
	Office staff	2	6 (12)	4 (8)	1 (2)	3 (6)	10 (20)	1 (2)	10 (20)
	Manual workers	3	7 (21)	4 (12)	1 (3)	2 (6)	10 (30)	1 (3)	10 (30)
Miscellaneous	Miscellaneous	5	5 (25)	5 (25)	5 (25)	5 (25)	5 (25)	5 (25)	10 (50)

the effectiveness of each of these activities when applied to the goals. The first number shown in each box is the effectiveness rating. The number in parentheses is the g-Factor.

In this example the practitioner has assigned an effectiveness rating of 10 against each goal under the heading "PR advice to board and management". This reflects an attitude that his/her principal contribution to the organisation can be at the policy-making level.

If for illustration we arbitrarily take a g-Factor of 60 as the dividing line between what should be undertaken and what shouldn't, Table 5 indicates that the PR programme should consist of:

> *National press*: Here the aim of press relations effort should be in the realm of spreading knowledge about the organisation and establishing its reputation.

> *Trade press*: Again this medium with g-Factors of 90, 80 and 60 is seen as valuable for achieving corporate recognition among certain groups. It can be effective also in stimulating sales (effectiveness ratings of 8 and 9) but as the PRP does not at the moment place a high priority on attracting *new* customers (priority rating = 4) too much effort should not be wasted on this latter aspect.

> *Corporate booklet*: This obviously merits inclusion in the programme provided the aims are confined to informing certain groups and establishing reputations.

> *Speakers' panels*: Same remarks as for "corporate booklet".

> *Corporate advice*: The g-Factors here are in direct proportion to the priority ratings, indicating that the PR practitioner would more profitably spend time by thinking about those goals which are near the top of the priority list.

Both local press relations and a company newspaper are seen as non-starters in the foreseeable future. Each is rated as very effective for one or more goal but these goals are not given a high priority.

Obviously the next step is to prepare a budget for these activities and to allocate staff time. If this programme still leaves spare staff and funds then other activities lower down the g-Factor table can be undertaken too.

Conclusion
The g-Factor is a useful device for helping practitioners to be more objective in their judgements when drawing up a plan of activities. It challenges them to assess clearly in their own minds which goals have

higher or lower priorities than others and to determine from their own experience which activities have the best or worst chances of success for achieving these goals.

Appendix 5. The Naming of Polytechnics (That Which We Would Call a Rose)

Clive Keen

The following is reprinted from Universities Quarterly *(now* Higher Education*), Spring 1986.*

The proposal to include *University* in the title of various polytechnics needs careful analysis now that the Association of Polytechnic Teachers has voted in its favour and the Chairman of the Board of the National Advisory Body has offered written support. Much discussion to date has centred on the *ad hominem*, with motives being questioned and insinuations made that an unseemly quest for prestige is the dominant factor. This has clarified nothing. Two things need to be closely examined. First, would a name change genuinely benefit polytechnics? Secondly, would it benefit higher education as a whole?

I propose to start with the first question, which is closest to home. In spite of some wishful thinking down at Portsmouth,[41] it is clear that the name change would affect only appearances, not realities such as funding. The only benefit to polytechnics in a name change, therefore, would result from altering public perceptions of their work. And this, of course, is the main idea. The "official" argument would run something like this:

> The public's understanding of polytechnics (as last summer's MORI poll showed) is lamentable; polytechnic graduates are grossly undervalued as a result; these graduates thus have an unfair handicap in the job market; retitling the polytechnics as universities would solve this at a stroke; this should therefore be done without delay.

The fact that this argument has been forwarded only by academics and administrators, and seems to have found little favour with polytechnic students, weakens its impact, but the argument has merits nevertheless. A name change certainly would help polytechnics with their image amongst the public at large, over half of which thinks that they teach hairdressing, plumbing and poodle-clipping. *Polytechnic* for such people is simply an alternative name for the local tech.

Careful readers of the MORI poll, however, will realise that polytechnics have two public relations problems, not one. The second image problem arises amongst the smaller proportion of the population (33%) that has a reasonable idea of what polytechnics do, appreciating, for example, that they actually teach degree courses. Amongst this group, there is a strong tendency to see polytechnics simply as places that students go to if they can't get into a university. Where this − rather more important − group is concerned, it is the "second-class university" image that causes worries.

Now a very good case can be made for the view that whereas retitling of polytechnics will help solve the first (hairdressing/plumbing/poodle-clipping) problem, it will make the second, much more difficult, problem intractable. Faced with the "second-class university" image, the strategy of the polytechnics has been to accentuate differences. The standard public relations message can be summarised as follows:

> Polytechnics and universities now provide, more successfully than the critics ever imagined, a genuinely complementary system of higher education. Each is capable of dealing successfully with a different type of student. Some young people are natural scholars − they are motivated by intellectual curiosity, and wish nothing better than to forward their own, and society's, understanding. For them, the university, with its commitment to primary research, is a perfect environment. Other highly capable young people, though, are much more sceptical about the notion of knowledge for knowledge's sake. For them, understanding is pointless unless it is directed to some practical end, and will be of clear value in their future careers. Such people are catered for directly by the polytechnics, which are teaching- and career-orientated, rather than institutions of primary research.

(Oxford Times, 25 January 1985)

This message is, of course, a simplification, but it provides the basis for a perfectly credible solution to the problem caused by polytechnics' lower A-level requirements, which are at the heart of the "second-class" image. *Of course*, polytechnics can say, they do not insist on high A-level scores − high A-level scores just indicate whether or not a person is a natural scholar. Polytechnics can argue, with a reasonable number of examples to back up the point, that students increasingly go to them, not as second best, but because of the realisation that the education offered is more appropriate to their specific nature and goals. This approach is undoubtedly good for everyone's morale; it also corresponds more closely to the facts than polytechnic lecturers, in moments of depression, sometimes think.

Now, if polytechnics were relabelled as universities, this whole public relations strategy would crumble. In reality, higher education would settle into a system in which there were forty-four universities proper, and thirty "teaching" universities. Even the predicted shift in the culture away from respect for intellect towards appreciation of productive and entrepreneurial skills would fail to be of benefit. Nor could much remain of the original high ideals of the polytechnic sector.

So much, then, for the question of whether a name change would benefit the polytechnic sector. Let us move on, therefore, to the second issue — whether a change of name would benefit higher education as a whole.

In favour of the name change, it could be argued that a multiplicity of names — college/institute of higher education; polytechnic; university, etc — only confuses the industrialist and general taxpayer. Polytechnics, furthermore, are now a great deal larger, more experienced in course design, with lecturers more highly qualified, than the average university of 1966, when polytechnics were first dreamt up. Why not, then, have a single title — *university* — for all institutions of size and maturity that are primarily concerned with degree-level courses?

Many university representatives will undoubtedly snort at this suggestion. To their credit, few have yet done so publicly and drawn the public sector's fire. To return the favour, I shall risk my career by stating their implicit argument, and suggesting that it is by no means foolish.

In a recent visit to one of the more mature universities, I came across a fresh reference to the university's "style and dignity". This was not mere levity or pomposity. What the university possesses in the public eye — and what other institutions undoubtedly envy — is an aura of learning; a certain mystique, somewhat akin to the religious, covering its own style of operation. It is this sense of the hallowed — this aura — which maintains the motivation of those engaged in work lacking obvious cash value; it is this aura and its overtones of the sacred and reverential which makes it acceptable for grown men to wear funny hats and gowns, and makes the term "professor" meaningful and natural. It is also — and this is the important point — this aura which allows the university to engage in certain activities without fear that it will be called to immediate account. It can still, even after the funding crises of the eighties, teach single honours philosophy courses, or courses in speculative astronomy; it can still speak of "continuing the pursuit of knowledge for its own sake" and "transmitting for posterity the riches of our culture" without intolerable fears of incurring a further swing of Sir Keith's axe.

Mock as many undoubtedly will, this aura is an invaluable commodity in protecting one element of the work of higher education — but it cannot be overstretched. Its overwork in North America, where "university" is the title given to the place of study of one-third of the relevant age group, has led to an inevitable devaluation of many traditional academic virtues. Studying with a sense of reverence for great men and their ideas becomes so much foolishness.

Attempting to transfer this aura to polytechnics through a name change would undoubtedly gratify individuals, but it would almost certainly lead to its overwork and subsequent loss of meaning. And do polytechnics, in any case, really need the aura? The study of classics, poetry, cosmology and epistemology need the support of a reverential culture; the study of hotel management, mechanical engineering and accountancy can get on rather more readily on their utility alone. Subjects taught in polytechnics and universities, of course, are rarely located so neatly at the poles of the vocational/non-vocational continuum, but public relations is built on clear-cut images, not on the subtleties of gentle gradations. Polytechnics cannot, in any event, take a defensible stand on paradigms too far towards the non-vocational pole, where the aura chiefly resides: a sensible public relations strategy, therefore, must be based on clear identification with paradigms earmarked by hard-headed utility; the quest for aura, being largely incompatible with this, must be passed over.

Appendix 6. The Naming of Polytechnics: Some Second Thoughts

Clive Keen

The following was originally written for Higher Education Quarterly *as a follow-up to the article reprinted as Appendix 5. Publication of the present book overtook the original plan.*

In a recent article in this Journal (*That Which We Would Call a Rose,* Spring 1986) I argued that moves to add the title "university" to polytechnics should be firmly resisted: that it would be a retrograde step, damaging the most effective public relations strategies of both the polytechnics and higher education in general. I hereby recant. Recantation does not, though, derive from recognition of previous flaws in logic, nor is it a case of crossing fingers and muttering *eppur si muove* to escape the hostility provoked by article number one. Rather, it is a case of recognising that a Hegelian synthesis of the opposing viewpoints is, in spite of all appearances, possible.

A brief summary of the previous article, which can be roughly compressed into the following three points, might be useful at this stage.

1. A MORI poll into attitudes towards polytechnics has demonstrated great public ignorance of their nature. Polytechnics are more often associated with "craft" (hairdressing, plumbing etc) courses than with degrees. As a result, polytechnic endeavours, and their graduates, are grossly undervalued.

2. Influential figures in the public sector of higher education, recognising the extent of public misperceptions, have argued that a decisive way of increasing public enlightenment would be to rename polytechnics; transfer of the title "university" would aid this enlightenment and correct a severe imbalance of esteem.

3. Appealing though the above may be as a solution to the problem of gross public ignorance, it would, however, make the second of the polytechnics' public relations problems intractable. This second problem, quite as serious as that of gross misunderstanding, lies in the fact that polytechnics can so easily be seen as nothing more than second-rate universities: places to send the youngsters to, with a sinking heart, if they don't get the A-level grades hoped for. The only solution to this problem is to continue developing a different "brand identity" for the polytechnics, accentuating their distinctive strengths: and for this, retention of a separate title is essential.

Much of the original line of reasoning is retained in the present article. It is still firmly believed that the polytechnics must retain a separate identity and must explain what they, as a distinct sector, stand for. Since writing the first article, though, the extent of public misunderstanding of polytechnics has become even more apparent than the first shock of MORI indicated, and the hope that it would be overcome naturally with the passing of time can now be seen as vain.

Anecdotal evidence to this effect has been piling up inexorably since the MORI poll was published. Prior to that poll, such stories could be laughed off; in the days since, it has become only too clear that they are far from isolated cases of stupidity. The local bus driver who says "which of the town's polytechnics do you want to go to?" should not be a cause for derision. The town has several colleges, after all, and his customers use "polytechnic" "technical college" and "FE college" interchangeably. The parent who has been coached for several years by a polytechnic lecturer about the nature of the institution, and nevertheless informs the lecturer that young Simon is now taking a welding course at "Reading Polytechnic", is not an unnaturally slow learner. When the parent saw on the letterhead "Reading College of Technology", he *understood* "Reading Polytechnic", because that seems to him nothing more than a useful abbreviation.

After several dozen such anecdotal cases, collected with much pain, it is becoming clear that polytechnics are mistaken in thinking that even 33% of the public has a general idea what they are doing. 33% of the MORI sample might seem to have "got it right" by recognising that polytechnics mount degree courses, but many will only have so answered because they think that *technical colleges* offer degree courses. For most, the mind skips straight from "polytechnic" to "technical college" and back again. Even when the difference is carefully explained, most members of the public will have forgotten it within a few days unless they have a specific need to remember. And only those in the trade have such a need.

Resolution of the confusion might not have been quite so difficult were it not for the fact that technical college students commonly refer to their college as "the Poly". I used to complain regularly to the local press over stories about "the Poly's champion plumbing student", or "the best hairdresser at the Poly." Complaints to those newspapers, though, showed that the reporters had been acting in good faith. The technical college students interviewed had said, quite categorically, that they were "at the Poly" − because that is the title they and their peers use for their place of study. Attempting to break them of this habit is quite as hopeless as the attempt to "correct" the use of the term *hopefully*. A word's meaning, Wittgenstein has taught us, is dictated by the way it is used, not by its relation to some ideal referent.

It begins to look, therefore, very much as though the term "polytechnic" will just no longer do. Seventeen years spent in the endeavour to gain understanding for the term have quite simply failed. It does not follow, nevertheless, that the seventeen years' attempt at developing a separate identity have been wasted. There is, in fact, a means of changing the title of polytechnics which will indicate to the public what the institutions actually do while retaining – in fact enhancing – the carefully nurtured "brand identity" for the sector.

This is where Tom Woolley of Oxford Polytechnic enters the scene with some inspired lateral thinking. A simplified version of his insight is as follows:

The thirty polytechnics could not be considered, as individual organisations, to be universities, since they do not possess charters. Their right to award degrees is derived from their association with the Council for National Academic Awards. If, however, we tried to explain their nature to someone from overseas, we would make great progress if we said that each is, as it were, a constituent part of a "National University" system. An American, used to State Universities, would very quickly grasp the concept and gain an adequate understanding of the sector. By the same token, however, the explanation would make surprisingly good sense to our own population: it is instantly obvious that any "constituent part of the National University" would be an institution of higher, as against further, education, and would gain the power to award its qualifications from association with that national organisation.

Amending the title of polytechnics in line with this concept would be quite straightforward. Some polytechnics might take a minimalist approach. Disliking name changes, they might just add the description "a constituent part of the National University" to their publicity material. Others, however, might feel that considerably greater benefit would be derived from making the association with the National University system explicit in the organisation's title. Oxford Polytechnic, for example, might thus be renamed "National University – Oxford", while Plymouth Polytechnic might become "National University – Plymouth". Yet others might adopt a formula including existing titles in parentheses, such as "National University at Coventry (Lanchester Polytechnic)."

The name change, therefore, could be effected fairly readily, at the individual decision of each polytechnic, once the Committee of Directors of Polytechnics decided that it was worthwhile and the main validators agreed. Some practical arrangements would of course need to be worked out – would the chairman of the CDP become the vice-chancellor of the National University, for instance? Would the charter of the CNAA need revision? Before letting the fiddly details put us off, though, we should appreciate the enormous benefits that would be gained from this simple change of title.

The first, most important, change would be the almost instant removal of the massive public ignorance of polytechnics. The findings of the MORI poll would be turned round overnight. Instead of 33% of the population assenting, rather doubtfully, to the proposition that polytechnics taught degree courses, 90% or more would assent with confidence. Such a change in perceptions would take many millions of pounds of Saatchi & Saatchi effort, and would then only enlighten those within Britain: overseas, people would remain as baffled as ever.

In the wake of public recognition of the general nature of polytechnics, morale amongst staff and students would improve dramatically. In a recent television drama, a daughter said to her father "you've never given mother a chance to develop a real career. Here she is at fifty, a polytechnic lecturer, where if she could only have concentrated she could easily have joined a university." It is a fact that the community as a whole feels polytechnic staff to be second rate — and it is not surprising, when most of the community thinks that a polytechnic lecturer teaches liberal studies to trainee meat packers, pottery to pensioners, or welding to delinquents. Once the nature of polytechnic work was understood, the imbalance of esteem for polytechnic staff and students would be corrected instantly, and much creative energy would be released.

A further benefit of the adoption of the title "National University" would be to diminish the unacceptable aspects of the binary[42] line. Some aspects of the binary line may be beneficial; the country is in fact served rather well through the existence of two complementary sectors of higher education. The binary line, however, once allied with public misunderstanding, has inevitably led to the two sides being resourced at very different levels. After all, why on earth *should* trainee meat packers need the same unit of resource as the honours degree students of universities? There would certainly be no votes in correcting the imbalance.

The binary line also leads to a great deal of silliness within higher education itself. At present, the two sectors just don't know how to talk to each other. Once the polytechnics were renamed, as constituent parts of the National University, they would be seen as they are — as a distinctive element of the higher education scene, but nevertheless a perfectly natural part of it. As the country's largest university by far, the National University could shake off the old diffidence, and would no longer expect polite condescension from the universities. The functional groups of polytechnic and university staff would even come to realise that their separation into mutually exclusive organisations defeated their purpose of exchanging ideas. The exclusion of British polytechnics from the Association of Commonwealth Universities – in spite of the fact that Ryerson Polytechnic of Canada, for instance, is a member – would also be seen as a curious artifice benefiting no-one.

The educational world would not be alone in benefiting from the new title. Industrialists would find that the baffling mass of different names, comprehensible only to the trade, was replaced instead by clarity. Some sense could even be made of the colleges and institutes of higher education, which currently fall outside nearly everyone's ken. In the new regime, any college of a certain size, with a certain proportion of CNAA and higher BTEC work, could use a title such as "an Associate College of the National University." Valuable clues as to its nature would thereby be gained; such colleges would cease to be Cinderellas, devoid of even the fuddled identity of the polytechnics.

There is vast power in a name. Those who think that names don't really matter are captives of a naive, and damaging, epistemology. General names – the philosophers' *universals* – provide the grid references of all our thinking. If we cannot make the grid references intelligible, if we insist on persevering with symbols known to lack the power to enlighten, then we have only ourselves to blame if everyone gets lost.

Appendix 7. A First Degree in PR?

This book, if it has performed its task at all well, should have shown that sound PR practice cannot just be picked up instantly by any competent newcomer, since it involves a complex mix of theory and experience. The experience could of course be built up gradually through the years, and personal reflection could gradually lead one towards conscious recognition of the underlying principles. This is likely to be a painfully slow process, though. PR is so rich a subject that enormous benefits can be gained from sharing the experience, and considering the theories, of others. It is not surprising therefore that both co-authors, who have spent much of their working lives in colleges, have been keenly interested in higher education's role in PR education. To date, regrettably, the role of higher education has been less than outstanding.

PR "education" in Britain is very largely carried out on the job. Large PR consultancies can often perform quite creditably in this, because they usually possess a significant number of employees able to pass on ideas and experience to the newcomer. The top ten PR firms in Britain, for instance, employed an average of 156 staff each in 1986,[43] and their various specialisms enable a worthwhile induction programme for new staff to take place. In the world of higher education, on the other hand, the PRP usually works alone or with a tiny staff, and too rarely brings prior PR experience to the role. Most individuals are taken on from other areas of educational administration, or from journalism. Very few college PRPs indeed will have taken, either before or during their employment, the Diploma of the CAM Foundation, which had been for long the only educational qualification in PR.[44]

Both of the co-authors have thus been led to put much thought into the potential for developing higher education's role in providing appropriate education and training of PR personnel. Workshops and short courses are part of the answer, helping considerably with development of motivation and skills, but they do not address the deeper issues of PR education. This has been evident to one of the authors for some years, including his period as chairman of the IPR's education committee. The other co-author has explored the potential of an undergraduate degree in public relations as a result of the unusual features of Oxford Polytechnic's modular course, which he spent five years explaining to a bemused public.

Most colleges thinking of launching a degree in public relations would be discouraged by the logistical problems. Courses need to be made available not just in the central theory and practice of public relations, and in closely related fields such as business administration, organisation and management, and statistics; there is also a need to offer options, at least, in areas such as English, design, communications, psychology, the media, publishing, politics, and law. Any new degree in public relations would also preferably need to be offered in association with a cognate area as a joint honours course, rather than as a single honours degree; it would in addition need to be a sandwich course,[45] since the IPR has made it clear that experience must be an essential part of PR education at this level.

These requirements would be beyond most traditional colleges, but are in fact grist to the mill of Oxford Polytechnic's modular course. This course, which is now followed by nearly three thousand degree students, involves selection of course units ("modules" − each equivalent to about a quarter of a term's work) from the 600 available. To ensure that students follow a coherent programme of study, these modules are arranged into 36 or so "fields" (subject areas), and most students combine two fields in their individual programme. A survey of the existing modules, however, showed that a substantial number are highly relevant to public relations. By the addition of only a few core and synoptic units, a coherent field in public relations could be created with ease, offering a wealth of relevant options. Combination with a relevant second field would also be straightforward. Students could combine a study of PR with, for example, business organisation, tourism, politics, publishing, English, psychology, or visual studies. Many other combinations would also be possible for those with specific interests, such as PR with law, music, anthropology, hotel management, or a modern language.

Oxford Polytechnic would have little difficulty, therefore, in introducing the first British undergraduate degree course in public relations. Together with Cranfield's MBA and Stirling's Postgraduate Diploma and MSc, it would complete a much-needed spectrum of academic study. There would, of course, need to be agreement that the PR profession would benefit from such a course, that it is a suitable subject for bachelor-level study, and that higher education would itself benefit by diverting resources to this new area.

Would PR benefit?
This is the main question for public relations practitioners; and the authors believe that the public relations profession would, in fact, be the main beneficiary of the development of PR as an undergraduate subject.

There can be little doubt that PR suffers, at present, from the lack both of full credibility as a profession, and lack of a really sound intellectual base. The two are intertwined. Once *marketing* came to be a standard degree-level subject, books by the shelf-load were written by theorists and top-flight practitioners. Before too long, academic journals also came to be devoted to the subject, and even in Britain the profession ceased to be treated as one for charlatans or enthusiastic amateurs. Whereas marketing in the 1960s often appealed to those with chutzpah and little else, the subject had become, in the 1980s, one of the most sought-after in higher education.[46]

In the absence of undergraduate degree courses in PR, however, the majority of texts which are available are essentially "how to" guides − practical manuals which typically skim the whole broad area of the subject. A few explore the subject in greater depth, but most aim at passing on tips and developing skills, thus making few contributions to deepened understanding. Existing journals, too, are mainly aimed at the busy practitioner, who has limited time and inclination to follow a complex, closely reasoned study. One of the few exceptions is the IPRA Review, the quarterly journal of the International Public Relations Association. While the body of knowledge remains at this general level, however, the profession cannot be expected to attain the standing it deserves, nor will it attract in sufficient quantity the high calibre of entrants appropriate to its challenges.

Is PR suitable for degree-level study?

Traditionalists within higher education would almost certainly insist that PR is simply not amenable to the study in depth which is the hallmark of degree-level work. Such traditionalists would be more than happy to see PR education restricted permanently to the diploma level, arguing that the CAM Foundation provides a wholly adequate education for subjects of this type. While not in any way meaning to undervalue the DipCAM − one of the co-authors is proud to have obtained the qualification − it is argued that it would be complemented by degree level study, just as the Diploma in Management Studies is complemented by honours degree courses in the topic. Public relations can provide great intellectual challenge − there is many a PhD waiting to be written on the subject, from numerous angles, such as epistemology, moral and social philosophy, psychology, business studies, and indeed all the social sciences. Other countries are conscious of this, and are building up academic expertise in the subject. Canada, for instance, now teaches undergraduate PR courses in both the English- and French-speaking parts of the country, and the US has had such courses for many years. In its early days as an academic discipline, PR would no doubt be dependent for much of its material on cognate disciplines. Over the years, though, a corpus of case histories and theory would grow, separate PR departments would be born, and the subject would gain paradigms of its own.

Would colleges benefit?

The first universities to teach degree-level engineering in the 19th century did so with considerable trepidation. The subject was not felt, somehow, to be "respectable", like history, theology, or the classics. Nevertheless, there was an inevitability about the subject's development within the academic world; the shift in the demands of the economy, and the need for highly trained personnel in the new area, made it irresistible. Countries, and colleges, that failed to recognise the shifting patterns in the economy failed to prosper and lost ground to those with more foresight.

The later years of the 20th century have been seeing a change to the structure of the economy quite as profound as that faced during the 19th, as the service industries take an ever-increasing share of the gross national product and the employment market. In the recent bleak times of higher education, those colleges which have recognised the trends have suffered less than those with a more traditional outlook. Business courses, for instance, which were once looked down upon as a distinctly dubious import from the United States, now draw exceedingly high application levels: Oxford Polytechnic is not unique in attracting 70 applicants for every place on its BA Business Studies course. Demand for graduates in subjects such as hotel management, similarly, has led to protection of their departments against the excesses of the cuts. It has become evident that in difficult times, innovative subjects like tourism, and even retail management, merit a slice of the financial cake, due in large part to the tremendous job prospects available to graduates in the subjects.

In such a context it should not be forgotten that the public relations profession has been growing at an annual compound rate of over 30% throughout the 1980s – and job prospects are decidedly good. Provision of degree-level courses in the subject may seem adventurous, but they are far from anti-academic. Colleges which provide the education appropriate to student employment, and provide the intellectual basis for the developing professions, are fulfilling an essential part of their proper role.

Appendix 8. Professional Organisations Relevant to College PR

Brief details of some of the main organisations relevant to college PRPs follow, arranged in alphabetical sequence.

British Association of Industrial Editors

The BAIE focuses exclusively on organisational communications: house newspapers or magazines, newsletters, video programmes, audio-visual productions, and bulletins. Its chief aims are: to develop the skills of members; to promote a regular exchange of ideas and experience; to provide education in all aspects of industrial editing; to convince organisations of the importance of effective communications; and to improve standards of organisational communications. It publishes a handbook, a monthly *BAIE News* and twice-yearly *BAIE Magazine*, and holds an annual convention and study conference.

Further details are available from the General Secretary, BAIE, 3 Locks Yard, High Street, Sevenoaks, Kent.

British Council

The British Council is an independent body which promotes Britain abroad, having offices in 82 countries. Higher education plays a major role in the Council's work, since foremost amongst its activities are: planning cultural tours of Great Britain; arranging programmes for visiting scholars; facilitating transfer of British technology abroad, and the promotion of British culture, education and literature. The Educational Counselling Service, financed by 80 British higher education institutions, aims at increasing the number of overseas students coming to Britain, and provides support for overseas students and visitors. A 22-strong management team organises submissions for the education and training elements of overseas development projects.

Further details can be obtained from the British Council, 10 Spring Gardens, London SW1A 2BN.

Central Office of Information

The COI provides publicity material for government departments and other publicly funded organisations. About half the staff are involved in overseas publicity for the Foreign and Commonwealth Office or the British Overseas Trade Board. The COI has 900 staff, making it the largest public relations organisation in Britain; most staff members have previous experience in journalism, advertising, film production, television, exhibitions, publications, graphic design, photography, radio, or market research.

The COI maintains a useful library of photographs on all aspects of British life, copies of which are made available at reasonable cost. Also available are a number of videos, many on free loan, which can be valuable to PRPs in a number of contexts. In COI's work of publicising British achievements, its staff are always keen to hear from college PRPs about stories that can be used. There are seven regional offices, in Newcastle, Manchester, Leeds, Birmingham, Cambridge, Bristol, and London, and the headquarters are at Hercules House, London SE1 7DU.

Central Organisations Group

COG is an informal grouping of central organisations concerned with the dissemination of information about higher education; it met for the first time in June 1987, and thus its *modus operandi* is still evolving. Groups invited to this meeting (the invitation list was recognised to be incomplete) were as follows:

ACFHE	(Association of Colleges of Further and Higher Education)
AVC	(Association of Voluntary Colleges)
BRIEF	(Not an acronym – an industry/education linking, or *Brief*ing service)
BTEC	(Business and Technician Education Council)
CDP	(Committee of Directors of Polytechnics)
CIHE	(Council for Industry and Higher Education)
COI	(Central Office of Information)
CNAA	(Council for National Academic Awards)
CVCP	(Committee of Vice-Chancellors and Principals of universities – *see UIU below*)
CWA	(Careers Writers' Association)
DES	(Department of Education and Science)
ECCTIS	(Educational Counselling and Credit Transfer Information Service)
FAST	(Forum for Access STudies)
HEIST	(Higher Education Information Services Trust)
ICO	(Institute of Careers Officers)
NACGT	(National Association of Careers and Guidance Teachers)
NAEGS	(National Association for Educational Guidance Services for Adults)
NATFHE	(National Association for Teachers in Further and Higher Education)
NCVQ	(National Council for Vocational Qualifications)

NIACE	(National Institute of Adult and Continuing Education)
OU	(Open University)
PCAS	(Polytechnic Central Admissions System)
PPRISC	(Polytechnic Public Relations and Information Services Conference)
SCETT	(Standing Committee for the Education and Training of Teachers)
SCOP	(Standing Conference of Principals of colleges and institutes of HE)
SCUIO	(Standing Conference of University Information Officers)
SRHE	(Society for Research into Higher Education)
UCACE	(Universities Council for Adult and Continuing Education)
UCCA	(Universities Central Council on Admissions)
UDACE	(Unit for the Development of Adult Continuing Education
UIU	(Universities Information Unit of the CVCP)

The purposes of the meetings, which the group agreed should take place quarterly, are to:

- Help such groups maintain links, and develop contacts
- Inform one another of forthcoming activities
- Avoid duplication of work
- See whether co-operation on specific activities would be beneficial
- Exchange ideas on matters of mutual interest

Further information about COG can be obtained from HEIST, at 13 West Bar, Banbury, Oxfordshire.

European Confederation of Public Relations (CERP)
CERP, which was founded in 1959, has consultative status with the Council of Europe and is recognised by UNESCO. It is an organisation which seeks to link and harmonize public relations policies and standards throughout Europe. Further details can be obtained from the IPR (see below), which has been an associate member since 1965.

European Universities' Public Relations and Information Officers Association.
EUPRIO provides a professional network of colleagues in universities throughout the European Community who are engaged in public re-

lations, information and related tasks. It was established in Brussels with the support of officials from the European Community in 1986. The aims of the association are:

- To promote the exchange of ideas and techniques of public relations and information for university institutions amongst its members;

- To create an infrastructure to assist members in their task as professional public relations and information officers within their institutions;

- To promote the professional excellence of all the members in their work, both within and beyond the European Community.

Full membership is open to press, public relations and information officers in university institutions in the European Community; *assistant membership* is open to those within universities interested in the fields of information and public relations but not themselves directly concerned professionally; and *associate membership* is open to colleagues outside the European Community and also to those engaged in press, public relations and information activities in non-university institutions within the European Community.

EUPRIO arranges meetings, issues a quarterly newsletter, and is involved in research programmes. Further information is available from the Vice-Chairman, Mrs Anne Lonsdale, Information Officer, University of Oxford, University Offices, Wellington Square, Oxford OX1 2JD.

Institute of Public Relations

The IPR, which was founded in 1948, is the sole body which regulates and represents individual professional practitioners in the UK and is by far the largest organisation of its kind in Europe. Its aims are to:

- Provide advice, information and opportunities for discussion on all aspects of PR work;

- Promote the development, recognition and understanding of public relations;

- Establish and prescribe standards of professional and ethical conduct and ensure the observance of those standards;

- Encourage attainment of professional academic qualifications;

- Maintain contacts with PR practitioners in the UK and throughout the world.

The Institute publishes a monthly newsletter and a quarterly journal *Public Relations*.

There are eleven regional groups which arrange their own meetings and other events in addition to those of the central IPR. The groups are: London and the South East; West Midlands; North East; North West; West of England; East Anglia; Scotland; Wessex; Northern Ireland; Wales; Yorkshire/Humberside.

The three application grades of membership are: *Student*, which is open to all those who at the time of application are over the age of 18 and who are engaged on an IPR-recognised course of study leading to an examination in public relations; *Associate*, which is open to all those who at the age of application are at least 21 years old and who work as bona-fide practitioners in public relations; and *Full Member*, which is open to individuals who are at the date of application at least 26 years old, and qualified to undertake the practice of public relations, and have at least five years substantial experience in the practice of public relations and show considerable breadth of experience. (Full membership is also available to applicants over 24 with 4 years substantial experience if they have been awarded a CAM Public Relations Diploma.)

Fellowships can be conferred by secret ballot of Council in recognition of distinguished public relations work.

Further information can be obtained from The Institute of Public Relations, Gate House, St John's Square, London, EC1M 4DH.

International Public Relations Association
IPRA, which was established in May 1955 at a meeting at Stratford upon Avon, aims to:

- Provide a channel for the exchange of ideas and professional experience for those engaged in public relations practice of international significance.

- Form a Rotary in which members at any time in need of advice and guidance may be assured of the goodwill and assistance of fellow members throughout the world.

- Foster the highest standards of public relations generally in all countries, and in particular in the international field.

- Further the practice of public relations in all parts of the world and to enhance its value and influence by the promotion of knowledge and understanding of its objects and methods both inside and outside the profession.

- Review and seek solutions to problems affecting public relations practice common to various countries, including such questions as the status of the profession, codes of professional ethics and qualifications to practise.

- Publish bulletins, journals or other publications, including an *International Who's Who in Public Relations*.

- Undertake such other activities as may be deemed likely to benefit members or to contribute to the advancement of public relations practice throughout the world.

Further information can be obtained from the IPRA Secretariat, 10 Rue de Conseil-General 1205, Geneva, Switzerland, or from 4 Hayes Court, Sunnyside, Wimbledon, London SW19 4SH.

PPRISC
The Polytechnic Public Relations and Information Services Conference was formed in the late seventies with a voting member from each of the 30 Polytechnics. Full membership is open to the individual with the major executant responsibility for public relations in each polytechnic, and associate membership may be conferred by the conference, and is available to institutions enjoying associate membership status of the Committee of Directors of Polytechnics. The goals of PPRISC are:

- to further the efficient performance of public relations work together with information and liaison services in polytechnics generally and individually by providing opportunities for those so engaged to meet and otherwise communicate and exchange ideas and information on topics of mutual interest;

- to aid the development and implementation of a corporate public relations strategy for polytechnics through the CDP;

- to encourage the professional development of its members both in the skills and techniques appropriate to their work and in the maintenance of professional standards.

PPRISC holds two full meetings per year − a one-day conference in the winter, held in London, and a two-day summer conference, usually held in one of the provincial polytechnics. The executive meet, on average, for an additional four days per year.

A membership list and indication of current activities is available from the Secretary, the name of whom (executive members serve for two years) can be obtained from polytechnic PRPs, or from HEIST.

Standing Conference of University Information Officers

The aims of SCUIO are:

- To help advance the cause of universities and higher education in the United Kingdom, particularly by encouraging the development of skills, expertise and knowledge of information and public relations officers, or other university officers charged with information and public relations duties in UK universities;

- To provide a forum for the exchange of views among such officers.

SCUIO meets twice a year, normally in central London at its spring meeting (one day), and in a provincial university during the autumn (three days).

The chairman, secretary and treasurer serve for one year, and are joined on the committee by representatives of each regional group. Information about the organisation's activities, and a membership list, are obtainable from the current secretary, the name of whom can be obtained from university PRPs, or from HEIST.

Appendix 9. The Nature of HEIST

What is HEIST?
The Higher Education Information Information Services Trust was established early in 1987 with financial support from the Business and Technician Education Council (BTEC), the Council for National Academic Awards (CNAA), and The National Association for Teachers in Further and Higher Education (NATFHE). Its objective is to provide assistance to those engaged in informational activities about higher education and the broad scope of post-18 education. In particular it concentrates on activities designed to enhance the level of understanding of the Polytechnic and College Sector of Higher Education while helping to explain the breadth and distinctiveness of its course provision.

The services being developed are in six main areas: research, central distribution of information, education and training, consultancy, publications, and co-operative informational programmes.

Research
Initial HEIST research involved contacting all schools and other centres to gain data about their information needs. The research programme is gradually being expanded so that the information needs of all groups connected with higher education can be systematically explored.

Central Distribution of Information
One of the first major tasks of HEIST was to help develop a scheme for the central distribution of prospectuses to schools, further education and technical colleges, careers advisers, central libraries, and other information centres. A pilot scheme conducted by Oxford Polytechnic demonstrated that such centralised distribution schemes allow substantial savings to be made while improving the level of service. Beginning in summer 1987, HEIST has distributed centrally prospectuses for the colleges and institutes of higher education, while acting as agent for the Polytechnic Central Admissions System in the distribution of polytechnic prospectuses.

Education and Training
HEIST introduced a series of workshops for all those involved in the dissemination of information about higher education, covering a number of subjects, such as internal communications, corporate identity, and media liaison. In association with the Further Education Staff

College, it also offers 3-day residential courses, at the headquarters of FESC at Blagdon, near Bristol.

Publications
A series of publications on all aspects of public relations practice in higher education is being produced, of which this book is an example.

Consultancies
HEIST will, by itself or with other consultants, or in association with FESC, arrange for specialists to visit individual colleges, to provide anything from one-day consultancies on specific topics, to in-depth audits involving a thorough review of the college's PR and/or marketing needs. A separate leaflet is available from HEIST outlining these services.

Informational Programmes
Research into the informational requirements of various groups inevitably leads to identification of the need for specific programmes of activity. Information is thus provided for existing groups to help them with the planning of their activities. Where desired by other groups, co-operative activities are also undertaken: HEIST takes a part in approaching funding bodies and other organisations in order to help specific projects get under way.

Appendix 10. Some Further Reading

There is now a great deal of American literature, and a reasonable amount of British, on the subject of public relations. For those with limited reading in the area, practically all books will prove useful provided they are approached with an open – even sceptical – mind. No author (even the present ones!) should be accepted as preaching the gospel. The following list, though, will prove a particularly useful start.

General

Black, Sam. **Practical Public Relations**. Pitman. *A standard introduction which has been reprinted through a number of editions.*

Haywood, Roger. **All about PR**. McGraw-Hill. *One of the best and most readable general introductions to the subject currently available, but somewhat biased towards a marketing interpretation of PR.*

Howard, Wilfred (Editor). **The Practice of Public Relations.** Heinemann. *A compendium of chapters from a number of experts.*

Jefkins, Frank. *Probably the most prolific UK author of books on public relations, advertising, and marketing. Many are highly practical. Library catalogues should be consulted for titles.*

Lloyd, Peter and Herbert. **Public Relations**. Hodder and Stroughton Teach Yourself Books. *A clear text which has deservedly been reprinted in 4 editions since 1963.*

Income Generation

Kelly, John, ed. **Boosting University Income**. CUA (Conference of University Administrators) Publications. *Very useful. Available from CUA publications, Whiteknights House, The University, Reading.*

Media Relations

MacShane, Denis. **Using the Media**. Pluto Press. *Don't let the union-activist slant put you off. This book is superb.*

Marketing

Davies, Peter, and Scribbins, Keith. **Marketing Further and Higher Education**. Longman for the Further Education Unit and Further Education Staff College. Available from Longman Resources Unit, 62 Hallfield Road, Layerthorpe, York. *A valuable introduction to marketing, indicating the applicability of the marketing perspective to further and higher education.*

Megson, Christine, and Baber, Michael. **Taking Education Further**. MSE Publications, 16 Percy Street, Stratford upon Avon. *An unusual source-and-inspiration book about marketing in the college context.*

Corporate Communications
Bernstein, David. **Corporate Image and Reality**. Holt Rinehart and Winston. *Highly readable and stimulating.*

Publications
Keen, Clive. **The College Prospectus**. PPRISC/SCUIO Publications. *Modesty forbids an evaluation, so factual details are given on the following page.*

Journals
IPRA Review. A quarterly published by IPRA covering issues from around the world, and available to non-members on subscription. *A journal which carries international PR contributions of substance.*

PR Week. A Rangenine Publication, free to PR officers. *Though its news is biased heavily towards the consultancy business, the publication is gradually evolving towards compulsory reading for all PRPs. Some of its contributed features are well worth cutting out and keeping for future reference.*

PR World. A Rangenine Publication, available on subscription from 100 Fleet Street, London EC4Y 1DE. *Though of interest to anyone wishing to broaden their views about PR practice, the publication seems directed particularly at those interested in international business communications.*

Public Relations. The quarterly journal of the Institute of Public Relations, distributed free to members and available on subscription to non-members. *Particularly useful for its case studies.*

Other Publications from HEIST

This book is the second in a series covering all aspects of college public relations. The first discussed the college prospectus, and future books are similarly to focus on practical subjects, such as internal communications, visual identity, and media relations. A number of publications are in preparation, covering all aspects of public relations practice in the educational context. Current information can be gained by contacting HEIST at 13 West Bar, Banbury, Oxfordshire. The following was available at the time of writing:

The College Prospectus by C N Keen

This 128-page monograph (£7.25, or £8.50 overseas, inclusive of post and packaging) is devoted entirely to the theme of improving the college's most important single promotional tool: its prospectus. The contents are reproduced below.

Footnotes

1. *PR Week*, 5–11 March 1987.

2. Roger Hayward, *All about PR*, McGraw Hill, page 34.

3. University Grants Committee – at the time of writing expected to be succeeded by the Universities Funding Committee. It is a body that receives money from the government and allocates it amongst the universities.

4. National Advisory Body – at the time of writing expected to be succeeded by the Polytechnics and Colleges Funding Council. Its function, in respect of the colleges of higher education and poly-technics, is analogous to the UGC/UFC (see above).

5. A review of the poll can be found in the *Times Higher Education Supplement* of 26 October 1984.

6. Universities Central Council on Admissions.

7. Polytechnic Central Admissions System.

8. UCCA limits applicants to 5 university choices.

9. PCAS restricts applicants to 4 choices of polytechnic.

10. Haywood, *op cit*, page 119.

11. Many MORI polls have substantiated this. The MORI Chairman, Robert Worcester, wrote in *The Times*, 7 November 1985: "It is generally true that familiarity breeds favourability, not contempt. The more knowledgeable people feel about a company, the better they regard it. Among the public there is a high correlation between how well people feel they know a company and how favourable they are towards it. This leads them to be more likely to buy its products, to try new products launched by it, to buy its shares, and, in this context, to apply for a job with it." The assertion "familiarity breeds favourability" is now known as "Worcester's Law"; fifty years of conducting polls have shown it to be true, according to Bob Worcester, nine times out of ten.

12. See the footnote above.

13. The "Harrington affair", during which PNL students attempted to keep a member of the National Front from attending classes, stayed in the news for an extended period.

14. Sir Keith Joseph was Education Secretary throughout a period which saw a substantial contraction in the numbers of students that universities were financed to enrol, and a substantial reduction in the level of resource per student in the polytechnic and college sector of higher education.

15. To give an example: a speech made by Steve Norris, MP for Oxford East, on his first visit to Oxford Polytechnic in 1984, showed that he had followed closely, and had accepted, arguments in the local newspapers about inequitable funding. His subsequent speech on the issue in the House of Commons was based partly on those arguments.

16. A 1987 government white paper on the future of higher education proposed taking the polytechnics, and many colleges of higher education, out of the control of local authorities.

17. Model one is a variation of a method suggested by Roger Hayward, *op cit*, page 28.

18. The relevance rating is clearly the most important single rating, but equal in importance to it, when deciding how much of the PRP's time should be spent on each audience, must be the relative effectiveness which any communication programme could be expected to have. The formula adopted reflects this parity exactly.

19. A word of caution should be given here about the limits of the validity of mathematical manipulation of the matrix ratings. Given their nature, it cannot be pretended that a goal/activity combination receiving a rating of (say) 50 is thereby proven to be exactly 'equal in worth' to two combinations which each receive a rating of 25. It would be folly to treat the ratings as anything more than general guides. Nevertheless, just as comparison between the ratings gives us useful guidance on the relative merit of each combination, so does comparison of the total scores give us a pointer to the overall value of activities.

20. Hayward, *op cit*, page 62.

21. A special report on corporate identity in *PR Week*, 4-10 June 1987, began with the words "Corporate identity can be defined as the visual manifestation of an organisation's personality." Many other writers, also, tend to use the expression "corporate identity" where this text uses "visual identity". That tendency, however, seems positively unhelpful. Most writers will agree, for instance, that an organisation's name is a major constituent of its "corporate ident-

ity", but names carry impressions far over and above those transmitted by the name's visual manifestations. People who have never come across any of the visual manifestations of an organisation will often still have formed views about its corporate identity. The two are therefore not equal. Visual identity certainly contributes to corporate identity, but the latter remains a broader notion.

22. As this chapter was being written, ICI had completed its placement of a contract for £3 million. Earlier visual identity programmes, such as that carried out for British Airways, have cost over £10 million.

23. Wally Olins, *The Corporate Personality*, Design Council, page 52.

24. To give an example: many of us, when we hear of "Slovenia", will immediately think of slovenliness. This won't be because, after mature consideration, we have decided what a scruffy lot the Slovenians are, but simply because slovenliness is the only thing we manage to associate with Slovenia – though the etymology of "slovenly" does not involve judgements about the habits of Slovens, but involves rather an unconnected Dutch word for negligence. The justice or injustice of the association is not taken into account during the mind's wanderings, however. It is a fact of human nature that we don't like our ideas to drift about singly: we try to file them away with other ideas which appear somehow related. As a result, our minds will always tend to move from "Slovenia" to "slovenly" to "disreputable bunch of Serbs" unless there are other primary associations which break the train, leading the mind off in different directions.

    A different train of thought could in fact very easily ensue from "Slovenia", since the Republic produces the finest of Yugoslavian wines. A public relations practitioner hired by the Slovenians could thus produce a remarkable transition in our feelings towards their homeland simply by ensuring that the facts about Slovenian wines were well understood. Whenever, subsequently, we thought of Slovenia, our minds would be directed towards quality, good living, and civilised pleasures; the tenuous connection with slovenliness would tend to fall away.

25. Colonel Sanders was the founder of a "southern chicken" restaurant chain taken over by a company which trades in Britain as Kentucky Fried Chicken (Great Britain) Ltd. It is interesting that though the Colonel publicly disagreed with some elements of the new chain's policies, leading to lawsuits against him, the company nevertheless retained his features as the company symbol.

26. The co-authors should not be thought to be advocates of this approach!

27. All these figures are as of July 1987.

28. Esselte Letraset Limited manufactures a number of aids for graphic artists, including a wide range of instant lettering.

29. Birmingham Polytechnic's identity programme, conducted at low cost through maximising the use of internal expertise, nevertheless led to some unpleasant media coverage. An initial article in a design magazine praising the design, and remarking on its economy, was picked up by *The Sun*, which went on to lampoon the polytechnic for "spending £10,000 on two words".

30. Thanks are due to Marilyn Seeckts for raising the points made in this paragraph.

31. The largest British PR company.

32. *PR Week*, 16–22 April 1987.

33. Ideas organisers, such as Caxton's "Brainstorm", allow a series of jottings to be structured and harmonised by making interconnections on the basis of word matches.

34. Wordprocessing software commonly includes a facility for checking spellings against a large built-in dictionary and an additional personal dictionary.

35. Stylecheckers analyze sentence structure, giving warnings on such matters as repetition of words and cumbersome prose.

36. Oracle (ITV) and Ceefax (BBC) are systems of information transmitted over the airwaves by the broadcasting organisations. The signals "piggyback" onto programme transmissions and provide several hundred "screens" of text, which can be displayed as desired on domestic television sets.

37. The Professional, Industrial and Commercial Updating Programme run by the Department of Education and Science.

38. The Materials And Resources Information Service.

39. The Educational Counselling and Credit Transfer Information Service.

40. Compact Disk – Read Only Memory

41. Portsmouth Polytechnic has been perhaps the most single-minded

advocate of a title change. A statement released by its Board of Governors included the following:

> It is the public's misconception of the work of and the role of polytechnics in general, as against that of the universities, that the Governing Body finds most worrying. It has become fearful of the effect this may have on the future funding of the institution .... There is a strong feeling that one way, perhaps the only way, of achieving parity of esteem for the public sector, is by adopting the title "university" ....

Portsmouth Polytechnic at one stage assumed that it might leave the public sector, to be funded by the UGC. It has adopted the use of the title "Professor" for some of its senior academic staff and has now made a number of professorial appointments.

42. Institutions of British higher education are financed, and administered, in one of two basically different ways, so that universities are referred to as being on one side of the "binary line", while the polytechnics and colleges/institutes of higher education are considered to be on the other side.

43. Source: *PR Week*, 16–22 March 1987.

44. The Communications, Advertising and Marketing Education Foundation Ltd was formed in 1969 with funding from the IPR, the Advertising Association and the Institute of Practitioners in Advertising. Its purpose was to conduct examinations and award qualifications acceptable to a range of related professions. The CAM Certificate in Communication Studies is awarded on the basis of examinations designed to show a broad understanding of public relations, marketing, advertising, media, research and behavioural studies, and communications. The CAM Diploma can be taken by specialising in public relations, advertising, media studies, or creative studies.

45. I.e. a course involving experience in the industry.

46. It is indicative of the appeal of the subject that in 1985-6 some 3,500 applications were received for 50 places on the Oxford Polytechnic BA in Business Studies course. In the same year, some 22% of *all* degree applicants to polytechnics were for business courses.

Index

190

191